Series/Number 07-086

LOGIT MODELING
Practical Applications

ALFRED DEMARIS
Bowling Green State University

SAGE PUBLICATIONS
International Educational and Professional Publisher
Newbury Park   London   New Delhi

For information address:

 SAGE Publications, Inc.
2455 Teller Road
Newbury Park, California 91320

SAGE Publications Ltd.
6 Bonhill Street
London EC2A 4PU
United Kingdom

SAGE Publications India Pvt. Ltd.
M-32 Market
Greater Kailash I
New Delhi 110 048 India

Printed in the United States of America

Library of Congress Catalog Card No. 89-043409

DeMaris, Alfred.
   Logit modeling: practical applications / Alfred DeMaris.
      p.   cm.—(A Sage university papers series. Quantitative
   applications in the social sciences; v. 86)
    Includes bibliographical references (p.   ).
    ISBN 0-8039-4377-6
    1. Econometric models. 2. Logits. I. Title. II. Series.
  HB141.D42 1992   92-9657
  330′.01′5195—dc20   CIP

95 10 9 8 7 6 5 4

Sage Production Editor: Judith L. Hunter

When citing a university paper, please use the proper form. Remember to cite the current Sage University Paper series title and include the paper number. One of the following formats can be adapted (depending on the style manual used):

(1) DEMARIS, A. (1992) Logit Modeling: Practical Applications. Sage University Paper series on Quantitative Applications in the Social Sciences, 07-086. Newbury Park, CA: Sage.

OR

(2) DeMaris, A. (1992) *Logit modeling: Practical applications* (Sage University Paper series on Quantitative Applications in the Social Sciences, series no. 07-086). Newbury Park, CA: Sage.

CONTENTS

SERIES EDITOR'S INTRODUCTION

Logit modeling represents a breakthrough in the methodology of social science research because it offers ways to more efficient estimation of models with multiple, categorical variables. The problems it promises to solve are not trivial. For example, suppose a survey researcher, call her Professor Green, wishes to examine the relationship between dependent variable Y (with three categories) and independent variable X (with seven categories), while controlling for variable Z (with four categories). Traditionally, she might construct a three-way cross-tabulation and struggle heroically to make sense of the frequency differences in this 84-cell table. Alternatively, she might abandon the tabular approach and estimate an ordinary regression equation, with Y held to be a linear function of X and Z. Of course, this regression approach also poses major difficulties in interpretation. However, from either analysis perspective—tables versus equations—proper application of logit techniques can strengthen inference.

In this monograph, Dr. DeMaris begins by describing the logit model in the context of the general loglinear model, moving its application from two-way to multidimensional tables. In the first half of the book, contingency table analysis is developed, aided by effective use of data from the General Social Survey for 1989. The particular dependent variable—the logit—is the log of the odds of voting for George Bush in 1988. The parameter estimates, then, can be understood in terms of odds ratios where, for one model, the odds of a Bush vote were estimated to be about four times as great for ideological moderates as for liberals.

As long as the variables are measured at the nominal or ordinal levels, the cross-tab format for logit modeling works well. However, if independent variables are continuous, then the more disaggregated logistic regression technique is favored. While it may sound different from the preceding contingency table analysis, the model form is not dissimilar. A data example explores the relationship of three continuous explanatory variables—population size, population growth, and literacy—to the log odds of a high murder rate (in a sample of 54 cities). The maximum likelihood estimates suggest, for instance, that a 1% population increase raises the odds of a high rate by almost 6%. Besides a comparative discussion of the substantive interpretation of coefficients (odds versus probabilities), DeMaris describes significance testing and goodness-of-fit measures for logistic regressions, not to mention the modeling of nonlinearity and interaction effects.

In the final chapter, logistic regression is extended to dependent variables with more than two categories, categories that may be either nominal or ordinal. The extension to polytomous logistic regression allows researchers to forsake the inefficiency of ordinary regression in such a case, as well as to avoid turning to discriminant analysis, with its unrealistic multivariate normal assumption.

In sum, logit modeling achieves a general purpose, serving whenever the measurement assumptions for classical multiple regression fail to be met, for either the independent or dependent variables. Obviously, given that achievement, Dr. DeMaris's practical explication deserves a big welcome.

—*Michael S. Lewis-Beck*
Series Editor

LOGIT MODELING
Practical Applications

ALFRED DEMARIS
Bowling Green State University

1. INTRODUCTION

Not too long ago, a variety of disparate techniques were needed to model a categorical dependent variable as a function of a set of explanatory variables. These techniques ranged from the repetitious elaboration of two-way cross-tabulations at fixed levels of the other predictors, to ordinary least squares (OLS) regression or discriminant analysis for a binary dependent variable, to discriminant analysis for a polytomous dependent variable with continuous predictors, to nonparametric techniques for the case in which the dependent variable was ordinal. However, in the last 20 years or so, the advent of loglinear modeling has revolutionized the multivariate analysis of categorical data. A special form of the general loglinear model, the logit model, has become increasingly important as a unifying framework for these analyses. This development has brought coherence to the problem by providing a single multivariate model having sufficient flexibility to handle contingency-table, and disaggregated, data, as well as sets of predictors measured at any combination of levels.

Logit analysis provides an interpretable linear model for a categorical response, and thus offers a number of advantages over previous techniques. Primary among these are model assumptions that are not as stringent as those for regression or discriminant analysis (see Klecka, 1980, and Lewis-Beck, 1980, for reviews of the assumptions required for discriminant analysis and linear regression, respectively), and the availability of various types of omnibus tests that are not possible in the standard cross-tabulation approach. Logit analysis, for example, provides a global test for the significance of a given predictor controlling for all other predictors in the model, as well as a test for the significance of a set of predictors, controlling for other effects. Moreover, the impact of a given predictor on the dependent variable, adjusted for other effects in the model, is nicely summarized by parameters that translate into odds ratios. As we shall see, these intuitively appealing parameters summarize the effects of predictors in a compact and elegant manner.

The "logit" itself, from which the technique derives its name, is the natural logarithm of the odds, or the "log odds" (the term *log* in this monograph will always refer to the natural logarithm). The odds indicate the relative probability of falling into one of two categories on some variable of interest. For example, if, in a population of married couples, the probability of divorce is .4 and the probability of remaining in marriage is .6, then the odds of getting divorced would be .4/.6 = .67. This means that couples are about two-thirds as likely to get divorced as they are to stay married. This interpretation is easily seen by solving for the probability of divorce in terms of the probability of staying married: .4 = (.67)(.6).

Typically, in the multivariate setting, we are interested not in the marginal, or unconditional, odds of divorce for the population as a whole, but rather in the conditional odds of divorce, given other characteristics. Suppose that we consider just those couples among whom both partners marry in their teens and neither partner has completed high school. We find that for this group, the probability of divorce is .68. Then the odds of divorce conditional on teenage marriage and having less than high school education are .68/.32 = 2.125. In other words, couples in this group are more than twice as likely to divorce as they are to remain married.

In logit modeling we would express the conditional log odds of divorce as a linear function of a set of explanatory variables such as age at marriage, education, race, whether the couple experienced a premarital pregnancy or premarital birth, and so forth. The model is similar to the linear regression model or the general linear model for ANOVA, except that the response is the log odds rather than a metric dependent variable. However, like other continuous dependent variables, the log odds also has a theoretical range of minus infinity to plus infinity.

I shall begin by considering the case in which all variables are treated as measured at the nominal level. In this instance, the data are typically expressed in terms of a multiway contingency table, showing the simultaneous cross-classification of respondents (or subjects, in the experimental situation) on the variables of interest in the study. Before presenting this model, however, I will review traditional cross-tabulation methodology, so that the reader can begin on familiar ground. I will then proceed in Chapter 2 to develop the general loglinear model for contingency tables, and show how the logit model is derived from the general loglinear model. Subsequent chapters will examine logit models for multidimensional tables (Chapter 3), as well as the varieties of logit models that are used when one has ordinal (Chapter 3) or continuous (Chapter 4) predictors, a polytomous dependent variable (Chapter 5), or an ordinal dependent variable (Chapter 5). Throughout this book, I shall illustrate the application of these techniques using a variety of real data sets. The Appendix, moreover, presents programs in BMDP, SPSS, and SAS that were used to fit these models to the data.

Analysis of a Two-Way Table

I will briefly review traditional cross-tabulation methodology for two-way tables using an example drawn from the General Social Survey (GSS) for 1989. The GSS is a yearly survey of the U.S. population that has been conducted since 1972 under the direction of the National Opinion Research Center at the University of Chicago. Each sample is a stratified, multistage area probability sample of clusters of households in the continental United States. The target population consists of English-speaking persons 18 years of age or over, living in noninstitutional arrangements (National Opinion Research Center, 1989).

For didactic purposes the focus here will be the presidential election of 1988, in which George Bush was elected over Michael Dukakis. The dependent variable is whether the respondent voted for Bush or Dukakis, among all those who voted for either Bush or Dukakis in that election. Three explanatory variables will be employed to predict vote choice: sex, education, and political views. Education is based on the number of years of formal schooling completed and is coded as 1 = less than 12 years, 2 = 12 years, 3 = between 13 and 15 years (some college), and 4 = 16 or more years (bachelor's degree or higher). Political views are coded as 1 = liberal, 2 = moderate, and 3 = conservative.[1]

We will begin by examining the relationship between political views (with categories $i = 1, 2, 3$) and vote choice (with categories $j = 1, 2$). These variables should be strongly related. During the 1988 election Bush and Dukakis were clearly in opposition in their views on a number of issues that typically divide liberals and conservatives. In particular, Bush was generally against abortion and additional taxes for social welfare programs, while being for a large defense budget, a firm stance in dealings with the Soviet Union, and a hard line against crime. For these reasons we would expect conservatives to have supported Bush and liberals to have supported Dukakis.

TABLE 1.1

Cross-Tabulation of Political Views With Vote Choice in the 1988
Presidential Election ($N = 906$)

| | Vote Choice | | |
Political Views	Dukakis	Bush	Total
Liberal	197	65	262
	(75.2)	(24.8)	
Moderate	148	186	334
	(44.3)	(55.7)	
Conservative	68	242	310
	(21.9)	(78.1)	
Total	413	493	906

NOTE: Table entries are cell frequencies. Row conditional percentages appear in parentheses.

Table 1.1 shows the cross-tabulation of political views by vote choice for the 906 voters in the sample, along with the conditional percentages voting for each candidate, given political views. Our expectations are borne out: 78% of those identifying themselves as conservatives voted for Bush, while only 25% of liberals did so. Here we are treating vote choice as dependent upon political views.

The traditional test for the independence of these variables in the population is Pearson's X^2 statistic, which is a function of the discrepancy between the observed frequencies in the cells of the table, the n_{ij}, and the estimated expected frequencies under independence, the $\hat{m}_{ij}$. The test statistic is

$$X^2 = \sum_{i,j}^{I,J} \frac{(n_{ij} - \hat{m}_{ij})^2}{\hat{m}_{ij}},$$

which, in the current example, equals 162.7. With two degrees of freedom (df), this is highly significant and suggests that the hypothesis of independence can be rejected.

While the Pearson X^2 statistic is widely used, another chi-squared test statistic that is less well known but much more important in logit modeling is the likelihood-ratio chi-squared statistic, G^2:

$$G^2 = 2 \sum_{i,j}^{I,J} n_{ij} \log \left(\frac{n_{ij}}{\hat{m}_{ij}} \right).$$

This statistic is also referred to a chi-squared table and, like X^2, has $(I - 1)(J - 1)$ degrees of freedom. In our example, G^2 is 170.54 with 2 df, which is, again, highly significant. Typically, X^2 and G^2 will be fairly close in value, and should give the same substantive results. This is because the sampling distribution of both statistics is asymptotically chi-squared. The term *asymptotically* refers to the fact that the sampling distributions of X^2 and G^2 become closer and closer, or "converge" to the chi-squared distribution, as the sample size gets larger and larger, approaching infinity. This convergence is fairly rapid for even moderate sample sizes, and therefore the chi-squared distribution gives a good approximation to the probabilities in the tails of these sampling distributions. A critical assumption for this to hold, however, is that the number of cells, IJ, is held constant. When all variables are categorical, this assumption is easily met. We shall see, however, that this assumption is not tenable when we have one or more continuous predictors.

Chi-Squared as a Goodness-of-Fit Test

According to either statistic, we would reject the null hypothesis of independence and accept the alternative: that political views and vote choice are related in the population. Usually, when we employ the chi-squared test, our interest is in rejecting the null hypothesis of independence. Therefore, we are looking for a significant test statistic. But, for a moment, let us look at the problem from the opposite perspective. Suppose that our "model" for the data is that political views and vote choice are independent. We wish to know whether this "independence model" fits the data well (in the next chapter we will see how to write this model in loglinear form). That is, we wish to know whether this more parsimonious description of the data—one that omits an association between the two variables—can account for the observed frequencies in the sample. Now we conduct the same tests, using either X^2 or G^2. But this time we are looking for a nonsignificant statistic, because that would imply that the expected frequencies under the model of independence are reasonably close to those observed in the table. In this context, X^2 and G^2 become "goodness-of-fit" tests that tell how well a given model fits the observed data. In our example, the model of independence has a very poor fit to the data, and therefore is rejected. In general, the larger the values of either statistic for a given model, the worse that model fits the observed data.

This latter approach to chi-squared tests is precisely the approach we will take in loglinear and logit modeling. We specify a parsimonious model for the data. We then estimate the expected frequencies for our multiway contingency table, under the assumption that the model is correct. We compare the observed and expected frequencies using G^2, and, if the statistic is nonsignificant, the model fits the data well. If it is significant, the model is rejected, and we must then consider why our model does not fit. In Chapter 3, we will examine model specification and goodness-of-fit in greater detail.

Measuring the Effects of Predictors

A final topic of interest in this introductory discussion concerns how to measure the impact of one variable on another. In linear regression, the unstandardized and standardized regression coefficients are widely used to interpret the manner in which a given predictor affects the response, controlling for a number of other predictors. In categorical data analysis, the "effect" of one variable upon another is best expressed in terms of odds ratios. In fact, we will see that in multivariate models, the odds ratio is analogous to the partial slope in linear regression.

The odds ratio is simply the ratio of two odds. For example, the sample odds of voting for Bush, given that one is conservative, are (242/310)/(68/310) = 242/68 = 3.56. Notice that the odds can be computed using either the observed frequencies or the observed conditional probabilities, because the marginal frequency of being conservative—310—cancels in each denominator. The sample odds of voting for Bush given that one is moderate or liberal are, respectively, (186/148) = 1.26 and (65/197) = .33. Now the odds ratio of voting for Bush, given conservative, as opposed to moderate, is (3.56/1.26) = 2.83. In other words, conservatives have odds of voting for Bush that are 2.83 times the odds for moderates. The odds ratio for moderates versus liberals is (1.26/.33) = 3.81, while for conservatives versus liberals it is (3.56/.33) = 10.79.

Although there are three possible odds ratios that can be formed for comparison purposes, notice that only two are independent. For example, once we know the odds ratios for conservatives versus moderates, and moderates versus liberals, the ratio for conservatives versus liberals is simply the product of the first two: 10.79 = (2.83)(3.81). This makes intuitive sense, in that the odds of voting for Bush are 3.81 times greater for moderates than for liberals, and the odds for conservatives are 2.83

times the odds for moderates. We might wish to know if all three comparisons are significant. That is, are the odds of voting for Bush significantly different for the three different political ideology groups? In the next chapter, I shall illustrate a multiple comparison procedure for odds that will answer this question.

2. LOGIT MODELS: THEORETICAL BACKGROUND

In Chapter 1, I discussed Table 1.1 from the standpoint of traditional cross-tabulation methodology, and introduced two measures with which the reader may not have already been familiar: G^2 and the odds ratio. In this chapter, I introduce the reader to the general loglinear model by presenting such a model for the data in Table 1.1. I then proceed to develop the general loglinear model for three-way tables, in order to introduce a special variant that is the subject of this monograph: the logit model. The remainder of the chapter is devoted to a discussion of distributional assumptions and estimation procedures for the logit modeling of contingency-table data, and the interpretation of model parameters in terms of odds ratios. The chapter concludes with a discussion of measures of predictive efficacy.

The Loglinear Model for Two-Way Tables

Let us reexpress the data in Table 1.1 in terms of the general loglinear model. This model makes no distinction between dependent and independent variables, but instead simply seeks to express the log expected cell frequency as an additive function of several "effects." To start with, note that the expected frequency for cell$_{ij}$ under the assumption of independence between two categorical variables can be expressed as follows:

$$m_{ij} = n\pi_{i+}\pi_{+j}, \qquad\qquad [1]$$

where n is the table total, π_{i+} is the marginal proportion in the ith row, and π_{+j} is the marginal proportion in the jth column. Now if we take the log of both sides, the equation becomes

$$\log m_{ij} = \log n + \log \pi_{i+} + \log \pi_{+j}.$$

The log expected cell frequency under independence is partitioned into the sum of a constant (log n) plus an effect associated with location in the ith category of the row variable (log π_{i+}), plus an effect associated with location in the jth category of the column variable (log π_{+j}). While this manipulation provides a rationale for the construction of a linear model for the log expected cell frequency, the right-hand side of this equation will be expressed in slightly different notation in the loglinear model.

The most complete possible model for a two-way table is the model of dependence between variables. To allow for association between the two variables, one additional term is added. In terms of our example, and in slightly altered notation, the model is

$$\log m_{ij} = \mu + \lambda_i^P + \lambda_j^C + \lambda_{ij}^{PC}. \qquad [2]$$

Once again, the log expected frequency in a given cell is partitioned into the sum of a constant (μ), an effect associated with being in the ith category of the row variable, political views (λ_i^P), and an effect associated with being in the jth category of the column variable, vote choice (λ_j^C). However, this model now has an additional association parameter, λ_{ij}^{PC}, that represents the joint effect of being cross-classified in category i of political views and category j of vote choice, over and above the individual effects of each variable. To see how this reflects the association between variables, we must take a closer look at how these parameters are defined.

The parameters in a loglinear model are defined in a way that ensures that we can get unique estimates for them. All of the parameters are defined as functions of the log expected frequencies, and are subject to certain constraints. To start with, μ is simply the average log expected frequency over all IJ cells of the table, and will therefore be referred to as the *grand mean*. For the complete model, the dependence model, it turns out that the estimated expected frequencies are exactly equal to the observed frequencies in the table. (The rules for estimating expected frequencies under a given model will be explained in greater detail below.) In our example, μ is (log 197 + log 65 + ... + log 242)/6 = 4.898.

The effect of being in a given category of the row variable (λ_i^P) is the difference between the average log expected frequency in that row and the grand mean. Hence the effect of being in the category liberal (λ_1^P) is therefore [(log 197 + log 65)/2] − 4.898 = 4.729 − 4.898 = −.169. Similarly, the effect of being moderate (λ_2^P) is [(log 148 + log 186)/2] −

$4.898 = 5.111 - 4.898 = .213$. The effect of being conservative (λ_3^P) is $[(\log 68 + \log 242)/2] - 4.898 = 4.854 - 4.898 = -.044$.

Several things should be noted here. First, each effect is a deviation from a mean—in this case, the grand mean. Moreover, the average of the three row means is itself equal to the grand mean, that is, $(4.729 + 5.111 + 4.854)/3 = 4.898$. If the marginal distribution on political views were such that roughly an equal number of respondents were liberal, moderate, and conservative, then each row mean would be about the same, and all would be equal to their average—the grand mean. In this case, all three lambdas would be zero. Hence the effects are to be interpreted as departures from what one would expect under the assumption of an equal distribution across the three categories. Thus, in our sample, there are relatively more moderates, and relatively fewer liberals or conservatives, than would be expected if the distribution were equal in each category. Third, the three lambdas sum to zero. This is a constraint required for identifiability of the parameters. It also implies that only two of the parameters are independent, or *free*, parameters that need to be estimated from the data. The third parameter is simply the negative of the sum of the first two; hence $-.044 = -(-.169 + .213)$.

The effect of being in a given category of the column variable, vote choice, is represented by λ_j^C. Because there are only two categories of vote choice, there is only one free parameter, and its estimate is the average log expected frequency in a given column minus the grand mean. Thus the effect of voting for Dukakis on the log expected cell frequency is $[(\log 197 + \log 148 + \log 68)/3] - 4.898 = 4.833 - 4.898 = -.065$. The effect of voting for Bush is just the negative of this, or .065. In loglinear modeling, the parameters associated with the marginal effects of each variable are called the *main effects* parameters.

The impact on the log expected cell frequency ($\log m_{ij}$) of the association between political views and vote choice is indicated by the *association* parameters, the λ_{ij}^{PC}. Each of these parameters represents the inability to fit the log expected cell frequency using only the marginal distributions of each variable and the grand mean. Were political views and vote choice to be completely unrelated, these would be sufficient to compute $\log m_{ij}$ for a given cell. However, the estimate of $\lambda_{11}^{PC} = \log 197 - [4.898 + (-.169) + (-.065)] = .619$. Thus the log expected frequency in cell$_{11}$ is higher by .619 than would be the case were these two variables completely unrelated. Table 2.1 shows the parameter estimates for the complete loglinear model for Table 1.1. As is evident, the association parameters indicate that the log expected

TABLE 2.1
Estimates for Saturated Loglinear Model of Table 1.1

Parameter	Estimate	Ratio to ASE
Grand mean	4.898	—
Choice		
Dukakis	−.065	−1.716
Bush	.065	1.716
Political views		
liberal	−.169	−3.026
moderate	.213	4.319
conservative	−.044	−.802
Political views by choice		
liberal, Dukakis	.619	11.062
liberal, Bush	−.619	−11.062
moderate, Dukakis	−.049	−1.000
moderate, Bush	.049	1.000
conservative, Dukakis	−.570	−10.407
conservative, Bush	.570	10.407

frequency is higher in $cell_{11}$ (liberal, Dukakis) and $cell_{32}$ (conservative, Bush) and lower in $cell_{12}$ (liberal, Bush) and $cell_{31}$ (conservative, Dukakis) than would be expected were these variables unrelated. This suggests, as already noted, that liberals were more likely to vote for Dukakis and conservatives were more likely to vote for Bush. Although there is some departure from what would be expected under independence for the cells involving moderates, it is very slight, compared with the other cells.

The number of free parameters contained in an association term (such as λ_{ij}^{PC}) is simply the product of the numbers of free parameters in each lower-order term from which it is composed (e.g., λ_i^P, λ_j^C). In this case, political views consists of two free parameters while vote choice consists of one. The association term therefore has $(2)(1) = 2$ free parameters that must be estimated from the data. Let us be clear, however, about the distinction between the total number of parameters that make up a term and the number of free parameters that comprise that term. The political views-by-vote choice association term consists of a total of $(3)(2) = 6$ parameters, one for each possible combination of the two variables. However, only 2 of them are free, in the sense that once these are known, all others are determined by them. This property arises from the fact that, like the main effects, the association parameters are departures from averages, and hence sum to zero over the levels of either variable.

The Saturated Model. In loglinear analysis, the units of analysis are not the individual respondents, but are instead the sample cell frequencies. These are the independent "bits" of information that all together represent the total degrees of freedom in the data. In our example, there are $IJ = 6$ degrees of freedom in the data. As we use the information in the data to estimate parameters, we are, in a sense, "using up" the information. If we estimate as many parameters as there are degrees of freedom in the data, we have what is referred to in loglinear analysis as a "saturated" model—that is, all of the degrees of freedom are used to estimate free parameters. Hence the dependence model is saturated, because we must estimate a total of 6 free parameters to specify it. This leaves no degrees of freedom for testing the goodness of fit of the model. Were we to calculate G^2, we would find that it equals zero, with zero degrees of freedom.

The saturated model always perfectly reproduces the cell frequencies. This can be easily verified by using the parameter estimates in Table 2.1 to compute the cell frequencies in Table 1.1. For example, the model predicts the log expected frequency in cell$_{11}$ to be $4.898 + (-.169) + (-.065) + (.619) = 5.283$. The expected frequency is then exp(5.283) = 197, which equals the observed frequency in that cell. The situation is analogous to a linear regression model for, say, 30 individuals, in which we use 29 predictors to account for the dependent variable. This model would also be saturated, because we would be using 30 parameters (29 plus the intercept) to model the score on some response for 30 individuals (the independent bits of information in regression). Here we would find that R^2 equals one, and that there would be no degrees of freedom for estimating error, and, hence, for testing the model.

The Model of Independence. The saturated model is, in most cases, of little interest because it provides no parsimony in describing the data—all possible effects are used to account for the expected cell frequencies. Instead, interest centers on one or more possible unsaturated models, in which certain effects are hypothesized to be nil. For example, the model of independence between political views and vote choice sets all of the association parameters (λ_{ij}^{PC}) to zero:

$$\log m_{ij} = \mu + \lambda_i^P + \lambda_j^C . \qquad [3]$$

This model has two degrees of freedom for testing fit, because we are fitting six cells with four free parameters. Generally, degrees of freedom for testing the fit of a model are equal to the total number of cells in the table minus the number of free parameters estimated to specify the model. As noted in Chapter 1, the independence model provides a very poor fit to the data. It is therefore necessary to include the association between political views and vote choice in order to describe the observed table accurately.

Estimating Expected Frequencies. The population parameters of the loglinear model are the grand mean and the lambdas associated with different effects. Our interest, of course, is in the estimation of those parameters using sample data. The technique commonly employed is the method of maximum likelihood, or ML (other techniques are possible, however; see Hanushek & Jackson, 1977, for a discussion of the generalized least squares approach to model estimation). In the contingency table setup, estimation of the parameters is accomplished by calculating the maximum likelihood estimates (MLEs) of the expected cell frequencies (the $\{m_{ij}\}$) under a given model. Because the parameters are functions of these expected cell frequencies, we can simply substitute the MLEs of the expected cell frequencies into the definitions for the parameters to arrive at the MLEs of the parameters.[2]

In order to employ ML, it is necessary that we know the probability distribution of the observed cell frequencies, the $\{n_{ij}\}$. That is, we must know the formula or function that specifies the probability associated with getting any particular set of values for the observed cell frequencies. For a given set of $\{n_{ij}\}$, this formula is a function only of the $\{m_{ij}\}$ and, of course, the parameters themselves, through the $\{m_{ij}\}$. Once we know this function, the MLEs of the $\{m_{ij}\}$ are those values of the $\{m_{ij}\}$ that maximize the value of the function, for a given set of sample data. In other words, the MLEs of the expected cell frequencies are those values for the expected frequencies that would have made the sample data (i.e., the $\{n_{ij}\}$) most likely to have been observed.

Distribution of the $\{n_{ij}\}$ Under Three Sampling Plans. Under any one of three sampling plans, the probability distribution of the observed cell frequencies is known. These plans are fairly exhaustive of the types of sampling methods that are most likely to be used in practice. The first plan is characteristic of surveys: We sample a fixed number of cases, and then cross-classify them according to their joint distribution on the variables of interest. Under this plan the $\{n_{ij}\}$ have the multinomial distribution. The second plan is similar except that the sample size is not fixed ahead of time. Instead, we gather data during a fixed interval of time, and the final sample size is a random variable. This results in a Poisson distribution for the $\{n_{ij}\}$. The third plan is characteristic of controlled experiments: We fix, ahead of time, the number of cases falling into different "treatments," and, within each, we observe the distribution on the dependent variable. Under this procedure, the $\{n_{ij}\}$ have the product multinomial distribution.

All three distributions are similar, in that they contain the same expression involving the $\{m_{ij}\}$:

$$\sum_{ij} n_{ij} \log m_{ij}.$$

Therefore, finding the values of the $\{m_{ij}\}$ that maximize this expression maximizes all three distribution functions. Consequently, all three sampling plans lead to the same estimates for the $\{m_{ij}\}$, and, hence, for the parameters. Thus it does not matter which of the three sampling plans was used to form a multiway contingency table. Under any of those described above, we would arrive at the same parameter estimates for a given model.

Estimating the expected frequencies under a given model is quite straightforward. The MLEs of the $\{m_{ij}\}$ are those unique cell frequencies that "fit," or sum to, the minimally sufficient marginal distributions required to specify any given model (Bishop, Fienberg, & Holland, 1975). To illustrate, the dependence model contains terms representing the grand mean, the main effects of political views and vote choice, and the association between political views and vote choice. In compact notation the model is (P, C, PC), indicating the marginal distributions that specify the model. More compactly, the model can be represented in terms of the minimally sufficient "marginal" distribution, (PC). This two-way distribution is all that is needed to represent the model, because the other marginal distributions for P and C can be obtained by collapsing the PC distribution over either variable. The $\{m_{ij}\}$ for this model are the observed cell frequencies because these are the only frequencies that sum to all three marginal distributions, the one-way marginals P and C, and the two-way marginal PC. While we do not usually think of the two-way table represented by PC as a marginal distribution, we will see that as we consider three-way and larger-dimension tables, such two-way distributions are indeed marginals, in the sense that they are produced by collapsing over one or more of the other variables in the table.

Now consider the model of independence, which can be represented by (P, C). These are the minimally sufficient marginals, or, simply, "the marginals" required to fit the model, because the PC term—that is, the set of parameters represented by this term—is assumed to be zero. For this model there is only one set of cell frequencies that will fit these marginals *while maintaining complete independence between political views and vote choice*. This set is, of course, given by equation 1 above, and the resulting expected frequencies are the MLEs.

For tables in larger dimensions, similar formulas for the expected frequencies under a given model can be written. In these instances, we say that the model is "direct" because it has a closed-form solution for the estimated expected frequencies. However, most models are indirect; estimates of the $\{m_{ij}\}$ cannot be obtained through simple formulas but must instead be produced through some iterative procedure such as Iterative Proportional Fitting as used by BMDP, or the Newton-Raphson technique used by SPSS. Regardless of the directness or indirectness of a given model, however, there is always a unique set of cell estimates that fits the minimally sufficient marginals of a model, and thereby satisfies the model constraints on the associations in the data. These are the MLEs of the expected cell frequencies.

Significance Tests for Individual Parameters. We have already seen how to test the goodness of fit of a model using G^2 or X^2. Moreover, we have seen that for a two-way table, both of these statistics are also tests of the null hypothesis that the set of parameters contained in the two-way association term are all simultaneously zero. In the next chapter we will explore tests for terms and sets of terms in more detail. For the moment, however, we consider the test for an individual parameter. For example, we noted above that the estimate of λ_{11}^{PC} is .619, indicating that the number of individuals in the cell (liberal, Dukakis) is substantially higher than would be expected under the independence of political views and vote choice. The question is, is it *significantly* higher than expected?

One reason for the popularity of ML estimation stems from the asymptotic properties of the resulting estimators. As the sample size increases toward infinity, the estimator is usually unbiased and con-

TABLE 2.2
Three-Way Cross-Tabulation of Political Views With Vote Choice
and Sex

| Political Views | Choice | Sex | | Total |
		Male	Female	
Liberal	Dukakis	89	108	197
	Bush	28	37	65
Moderate	Dukakis	58	90	148
	Bush	72	114	186
Conservative	Dukakis	27	41	68
	Bush	120	122	242
Total		394	512	906

verges in value to the population parameter. Moreover, its sampling distribution approaches normality, and its variance is the lowest among all asymptotically unbiased estimators. Therefore, for large samples, the test for whether a given parameter equals zero is approximately a z test, obtained by taking the ratio of the parameter estimate to its asymptotic standard error (ASE), where ASE is the square root of the variance of the parameter estimate. (Some analysts advocate a t test to be conservative—e.g., Aldrich & Nelson, 1984—but, because the t distribution converges to the z distribution asymptotically, use of the z test is appropriate in large samples.) For λ_{11}^{PC}, the test is .619/.056 = 11.05, which is highly significant. The column headed "Ratio to ASE" in Table 2.1 presents the z tests for all parameters in the saturated model for the two-way cross-tabulation in Table 1.1. Ratios of 1.96 or larger can be considered significant.

The Loglinear Model for Three-Way Tables

We now consider the three-way contingency table formed by adding respondent's sex to the cross-tabulation of political views and vote choice. The new table is presented in Table 2.2, and is arranged so that for each of the i ($i = 1, 2, 3$) levels of political views, the jth level of vote choice ($j = 1, 2$) is cross-tabulated with the kth level of sex ($k = 1, 2$). The saturated loglinear model for this table is as follows:

$$\log m_{ijk} = \mu + \lambda_i^P + \lambda_j^C + \lambda_k^S + \lambda_{ij}^{PC} + \lambda_{ik}^{PS} + \lambda_{jk}^{CS} + \lambda_{ijk}^{PCS}. \quad [4]$$

With the addition of one variable, the model has become considerably more complex. There are now three main effects terms (P, C, and S) and three terms representing associations between pairs of variables in the table: political views and vote choice (PC), political views and sex (PS), and vote choice and sex (CS). Finally, there is a term that represents the three-way interaction among political views, vote choice, and sex (PCS). Were we to consider vote choice the dependent variable, this last term would represent the first-order interaction of political views and sex in their effects on vote choice. As before, all parameters sum to zero over any of the indexes in their subscripts: i, j, or k. Table 2.3 shows the parameter estimates and ratios of estimates to their ASEs for this model.

Each set of two-way association parameters represents the conditional association between two variables, given the third. In other words, as in a regression model, each two-way term represents the association between a given pair of variables, controlling for the third. The z tests for the parameter estimates (estimate/ASE) suggest that the only significant two-way effects have to do with the association between political views and vote choice. The nature of this association is essentially unchanged after controlling for sex of respondent. It is still the case that there are more observations in the cells (liberal, Dukakis) and (conservative, Bush) than would be expected under independence; that is, liberals tended to vote for Dukakis and conservatives tended to vote for Bush.

The other two-way associations suggest that males were more likely than females to vote for Bush, and that males were more likely than females to identify themselves as either liberals or conservatives, while females were more likely to identify themselves as moderates. However, none of the z tests for these parameter estimates reached significance.

The parameter estimates for the first-order interaction between political views and sex in their effects on vote choice represent departures from what would be expected under the hypothesis of no first-order interaction. That is, they are departures from the case in which the association between any pair of variables is constant over levels of the third variable. In our example, they suggest that for liberals and moderates there are relatively more observations in the cells (male, Dukakis) and (female, Bush), while for conservatives there are relatively more observations in the cells (male, Bush) and (female, Dukakis), than would be expected were there no three-way interaction present.

In this instance, these trends coincide with the fact that liberal and moderate males have lower odds of voting for Bush than their female

TABLE 2.3

Saturated Loglinear Parameter Estimates for Table 2.2

Parameter	Estimate	Ratio to ASE
Grand mean	4.191	—
Sex		
male	−.150	−3.919
female	.150	3.919
Choice		
Dukakis	−.067	−1.752
Bush	.067	1.752
Political views		
liberal	−.162	−2.864
moderate	.203	4.023
conservative	−.040	−.726
Choice by sex		
Dukakis, male	−.025	−.642
Dukakis, female	.025	.642
Bush, male	.025	.642
Bush, female	−.025	−.642
Political views by sex		
liberal, male	.032	.572
liberal, female	−.032	−.572
moderate, male	−.074	−1.475
moderate, female	.074	1.475
conservative, male	.042	.753
conservative, female	−.042	−.753
Political views by choice		
liberal, Dukakis	.624	11.021
liberal, Bush	−.624	−11.021
moderate, Dukakis	−.046	−.911
moderate, Bush	.046	.911
conservative, Dukakis	−.578	−10.390
conservative, Bush	.578	10.390
Political views by choice by sex		
liberal, Dukakis, male	.046	.811
liberal, Dukakis, female	−.046	−.811
liberal, Bush, male	−.046	−.811
liberal, Bush, female	.046	.811
moderate, Dukakis, male	.030	.590
moderate, Dukakis, female	−.030	−.590
moderate, Bush, male	−.030	−.590
moderate, Bush, female	.030	.590
conservative, Dukakis, male	−.076	−1.359
conservative, Dukakis, female	.076	1.359
conservative, Bush, male	.076	1.359
conservative, Bush, female	−.076	−1.359

counterparts, while conservative males have greater odds of voting for Bush. This is evident upon examination of the expected frequencies in Table 2.2. (Recall that expected frequencies equal observed frequencies for saturated models.) If we define the odds in terms of voting for Bush over Dukakis, then the odds ratio for males versus females is [(28/89)/(37/108)] = .92 for liberals, [(72/58)/(114/90)] = .98 for moderates, and [(120/27)/(122/41)] = 1.49 for conservatives. Although these parameter estimates are not significant, they are suggestive of a disordinal interaction (Jaccard, Turrisi, & Wan, 1990) between political views and sex in their effects on vote choice. That is, the relationship between sex and vote choice changes in nature, or direction, across levels of political views.

The Logit Model for a Three-Way Table

The parameter estimates for the loglinear model indicate the effects of variables singly or in combination with others on log expected cell frequencies. As we have seen, these estimates have only limited interpretive appeal. Moreover, we typically wish to focus on one variable as being dependent upon the others. Loglinear models make no such distinctions. Therefore, from now on we will focus on the logit model, in which one variable is chosen as the dependent variable. As noted before, the logit is simply the log of the odds of being in one versus another category of the dependent variable. In our example, vote choice will be the dependent variable, and we will focus on the odds of voting for Bush (category $j = 2$ of vote choice) rather than Dukakis (category $j = 1$ of vote choice). The logit model is developed by manipulating the loglinear model as follows. Take the log odds of voting for Bush, conditional on the ith category of political views and the kth category of sex. That is, take $\log(\pi_{i2k}/\pi_{i1k})$, which, as noted in Chapter 1, is the same as $\log(m_{i2k}/m_{i1k})$. We have

$$\log \frac{m_{i2k}}{m_{i1k}} = \log m_{i2k} - \log m_{i1k} \, ,$$

which, after substituting the saturated loglinear model parameters for $\log m_{i2k}$ and $\log m_{i1k}$, equals

$$\mu + \lambda_i^P + \lambda_2^C + \lambda_k^S + \lambda_{i2}^{PC} + \lambda_{ik}^{PS} + \lambda_{2k}^{CS} + \lambda_{i2k}^{PCS}$$

$$- (\mu + \lambda_i^P + \lambda_1^C + \lambda_k^S + \lambda_{i1}^{PC} + \lambda_{ik}^{PS} + \lambda_{1k}^{CS} + \lambda_{i1k}^{PCS}) \, ,$$

which, after canceling like terms and collecting terms, equals

$$(\lambda_2^C - \lambda_1^C) + (\lambda_{i2}^{PC} - \lambda_{i1}^{PC}) + (\lambda_{2k}^{CS} - \lambda_{1k}^{CS}) + (\lambda_{i2k}^{PCS} - \lambda_{i1k}^{PCS}). \qquad [5]$$

This expression can be further simplified, by recalling that parameter estimates sum to zero across categories of vote choice. Thus $\lambda_1^C + \lambda_2^C = 0$, which implies that $\lambda_1^C = -\lambda_2^C$. Hence,

$$\lambda_2^C - \lambda_1^C = \lambda_2^C - (-\lambda_2^C) = 2\lambda_2^C.$$

Similar reductions apply to the other terms in equation 5, so that our logit model becomes

$$\log \frac{m_{i2k}}{m_{i1k}} = 2\lambda_2^C + 2\lambda_{i2}^{PC} + 2\lambda_{2k}^{CS} + 2\lambda_{i2k}^{PCS}. \qquad [6]$$

Finally, the logit model is written in slightly altered notation, reflecting which terms are constants and which are functions of the independent variables. Moreover, the odds will be more compactly expressed with the notation O_2^C, which represents the odds of being in category 2 (as opposed to category 1—the only other possibility) of (vote) choice. The logit model is then

$$\log O_2^C = \alpha + \tau_i^P + \tau_k^S + \tau_{ik}^{PS}. \qquad [7]$$

The parameter estimates for Equation 7 are seen in Equation 6 to be simply twice the values of selected parameter estimates from Table 2.3. For example, the intercept in Equation 7 is $2\lambda_2^C = 2(.067) = .134$. Similarly, the estimate of τ_1^P is $2\lambda_{12}^{PC} = 2(-.624) = -1.248$; while the estimate for τ_{32}^{PS} is $2\lambda_{322}^{PCS} = 2(-.076) = -.152$, and so on. Table 2.4 shows the parameter estimates for the logit model. These are given in the column headed "Additive Estimate" in panel A of the table.

Because the response is now the log odds, logit model parameters have a different interpretation from those in the loglinear model. The intercept, alpha, is now the average log odds over all ik levels of the predictors—that is, over all $(3)(2) = 6$ combinations of levels of political views and sex. The association parameters, the taus, reflect the effects of variables or combinations of variables on the log odds of voting for Bush. The main effects of political views and sex are represented

TABLE 2.4

Logit Model of Vote Choice as a Function of Sex and Political Ideology, Based on Data in Table 2.2

A. Parameter Estimates

Effect		Additive Estimate	Multiplicative Estimate	Ratio to ASE
Intercept		.134	1.143	1.752
Sex				
male		.05	1.051	.642
female		−.05	.951	−.642
Polviews				
liberal		−1.248	.287	−11.020
moderate		.092	1.096	.911
conservative		1.156	3.177	10.390
Polviews * sex				
liberal	male	−.092	.912	−.811
	female	.092	1.096	.811
moderate	male	−.060	.942	−.590
	female	.060	1.062	.590
conservative	male	.152	1.164	1.359
	female	−.152	.859	−1.359

B. Predicted Odds of Voting for Bush for Levels of Political Views, by Sex

	Liberal	Moderate	Conservative
Males	.315	1.241	4.446
Females	.342	1.266	2.968

C. Odds Ratios for Males Versus Females, by Political Views

	Liberal	Moderate	Conservative
Odds ratio	.920	.980	1.498

by τ_i^P and τ_k^S, respectively, while the first-order interaction of political views and sex in their effects on the log odds is represented by τ_{ik}^{PS}.

Values of main and interaction effects are interpreted as increments or decrements to the log odds relative to what would be expected were there no association between a given predictor (or combination of predictors, in the case of interaction) and the log odds. Thus being male is estimated to raise the log odds of voting for Bush by about .05, compared with what would be expected were there no association between sex and vote choice. Being liberal decreases the log odds substantially, and being conservative increases the log odds substantially, compared with what would be expected were vote choice independent of political views. Finally, the first-order interaction parameter estimates suggest that among liberals and moderates being male decreases the log odds, while among conservatives being male increases the log odds, over and above what would be expected were there no interaction effects present.

The interaction effect can be seen more readily by calculating the predicted odds of voting for Bush for each level of political views, separately by sex. This can be done using the estimates themselves. One simply substitutes the appropriate estimates into Equation 7, calculates the log odds, and then exponentiates to recover the odds. For example, the predicted log odds of voting for Bush for liberal males is .134 + .05 − 1.248 − .092 = −1.156. The predicted odds are then exp(−1.156) = .315. The predicted odds are presented in panel B of Table 2.4. The interaction can be seen from two perspectives. First, we notice that the impact of changing from liberal to moderate to conservative produces a larger difference among males, compared with females (.315 to 4.446, compared with .342 to 2.968, respectively). Second, we notice that the odds of voting for Bush are lower among males, compared with females, for both liberals and moderates. For conservatives, however, the opposite is true. This is shown in panel C of Table 2.4, where I have calculated the odds ratios for males versus females, based on the figures in the immediately preceding columns.

The significance tests for the logit parameters are the same as those for the corresponding loglinear parameters. In that tau = twice lambda for any given tau parameter estimate, the standard error of tau is just twice the standard error of lambda. The z tests for the parameter estimates are in the column headed "Ratio to ASE" in panel A of the table. As before, we notice that the only significant effect in the data is the relationship between political views and vote choice.

Note that in Equation 7 there are no terms reflecting associations among only the independent variables, because these terms cancel out in the transition from the loglinear to the logit model. However, these effects are still incorporated into the logit model, by virtue of the fact that the logit model is estimated by estimating the corresponding loglinear model that includes these associations. In fact, in logit modeling it will always be the case that the model is estimated by estimating the corresponding loglinear model that contains all possible associations among the predictors. These terms must be included because in logit modeling the predictors are treated as though they were fixed by design.

Hence associations among them are not subject to test. Their marginal distributions must always be fitted in the model exactly as they are observed. In this manner, any lack of fit of the model to the data will never be due to the failure to incorporate the associations among the predictors, but only to the inability to account effectively for the associations between the predictors and the dependent variable.

The Multiplicative Model. If we exponentiate both sides of Equation 7, we have

$$\exp{(\log O_2^C)} = \exp{(\alpha + \tau_i^P + \tau_k^S + \tau_{ik}^{PS})}$$

or

$$O_2^C = (e^\alpha)(e^{\tau_i^P})(e^{\tau_k^S})(e^{\tau_{ik}^{PS}}) . \qquad [8]$$

Equation 8 is the multiplicative model for the odds. Thus if we exponentiate each parameter and multiply together the resulting terms we get the predicted odds directly. The column headed "Multiplicative Estimate" in panel A of Table 2.4 presents the additive estimates in their multiplicative ($\exp[\tau]$) form. Multiplicative estimates greater than 1 indicate that a given category of a predictor (or predictors) is associated with an increase in the odds. For example, the estimate of 3.177 for category 3 (being conservative) of political views indicates that conservatives have odds of voting for Bush that are 3.177 times what would be expected were political views unrelated to vote choice. Estimates less than 1 indicate a corresponding decrease in the odds, while estimates close to 1 indicate no effect on the odds. Regardless of which column we use to recover the estimated odds, the result will agree with the odds calculated using the observed table frequencies, because we have estimated the saturated logit model. The G^2 and df for this model (both equal to zero) are the same as those for the saturated loglinear model used to estimate it.

A More Parsimonious Model. Because the only significant effect on the logit of vote choice in Table 2.4 (panel A) was the main effect of political ideology, the most parsimonious logit model for the data in Table 2.2 is

$$\log O_{\text{BUSH}}^C = \alpha + \tau_i^P . \qquad [9]$$

TABLE 2.5

Logit Model of Vote Choice as a Function of Political Ideology:
Parameter Estimates and Expected Frequencies

A. Parameter Estimates

Effect	Additive Estimate	Multiplicative Estimate	Ratio to ASE
Intercept	.130	1.139	1.716
Polviews			
liberal	−1.238	.290	−11.062
moderate	.098	1.103	1.000
conservative	1.140	3.127	10.407

B. Expected Frequencies

Political Views	Choice	Male	Female	Total
			Sex	
Liberal	Dukakis	87.97	109.03	197.0
	Bush	29.03	35.97	65.0
Moderate	Dukakis	57.60	90.40	148.0
	Bush	72.40	113.60	186.0
Conservative	Dukakis	32.25	35.75	68.0
	Bush	114.75	127.25	242.0
Total		394.0	512.0	906.0

Table A.1 in the Appendix shows the SPSS program and associated output for the estimation of this model. It has a good fit, with a G^2 (not shown) of 2.19 (df = 3, p = .534). For ease in the recovery of logit parameter estimates, vote choice was recoded for the program so that "Bush" is category 1 (SPSS does not print estimates associated with the last category of any variable, as these are mathematically redundant). The parameter estimates for the model in Equation 9 are $\alpha = 2\lambda_1^C = 2(.065) = .130$, $\tau_1^P = 2\lambda_{11}^{PC} = 2(-.619) = -1.238$, $\tau_2^P = 2\lambda_{21}^{PC} = 2(.049) = .098$, and $\tau_3^P = -(-1.238 + .098) = 1.140$. Table 2.5 lists these parameter estimates, along with the MLEs of the expected frequencies under the current model.

Parameter Interpretation in Terms of Odds Ratios

Parameter estimates are readily interpreted in terms of odds ratios. For example, consider the odds ratio of voting for Bush for moderates versus liberals. We let O_{12}^{CP} represent the odds of voting for Bush given that the respondent is moderate, and O_{11}^{CP} represent the corresponding odds for liberals. Then, based on Equation 9, the estimated odds ratio, in terms of the parameter estimates, is

$$\frac{\hat{O}_{12}^{CP}}{\hat{O}_{11}^{CP}} = \frac{e^{\hat{\alpha}}\, e^{\hat{\tau}_2^P}}{e^{\hat{\alpha}}\, e^{\hat{\tau}_1^P}} = e^{\hat{\tau}_2^P - \hat{\tau}_1^P} = e^{[0.098 - (-1.238)]} = 3.804.$$

The odds of voting for Bush are therefore estimated to be almost four times as high for moderates as they are for liberals. Similarly, the estimated odds ratio for conservatives versus moderates is exp(1.14 − .098) = 2.835, while the estimated odds ratio for conservatives versus liberals is exp[1.14 − (−1.238)] = 10.783. As these computations reveal, if we exponentiate the difference between parameter estimates for any two levels of a predictor, we arrive at an estimate of the corresponding odds ratio for individuals in the first level versus the second. Moreover, this holds true regardless of how many other predictors are in the model. As long as we hold the levels of the other predictors constant, it is easy to see that these terms will be the same in the numerator and the denominator of the expression above, and hence will cancel.

Additionally, the odds ratios arrived at by exponentiating the differences in parameter estimates must agree with the expected frequencies. This provides a check on our calculations. Again, turning to our example, we found that the odds ratio for moderates versus liberals was about 3.8. From the expected frequencies in the table, the odds ratio is [(72.4/57.6)/(29.03/87.97)] = 3.81 for males and [(113.6/90.4)/(35.97/109.03)] = 3.81 for females. The odds ratios are the same for both sexes because Equation 9 posits the association between vote choice and political views to be invariant over gender.

Pairwise Comparisons of Odds

As I have suggested, Equation 9 is analogous to the general linear model for ANOVA, except that the response is the log odds of voting for Bush. Once it is clear that political ideology is a significant predictor of vote choice, we want to know if the odds of voting for Bush are significantly different across the three levels of political views. To test the null hypothesis that a given pair of odds is equal (or, equivalently, that their ratio is equal to one), we must test that the difference in the corresponding tau parameters is zero. Recall that the MLEs are asymptotically normal and unbiased. Therefore, for large samples the estimates of the taus are approximately normal, implying that their differences are also approximately normal, with mean equal to the differences in the corresponding parameters. So a test of whether the odds of voting for Bush are different for moderates and liberals is a test of the null hypothesis that $\tau_2^P - \tau_1^P = 0$. The test is

$$z = \frac{\hat{\tau}_2^P - \hat{\tau}_1^P}{SE(\hat{\tau}_2^P - \hat{\tau}_1^P)} .$$

Unfortunately, the estimated standard error of the difference between tau estimates—the term in the denominator—is not provided by most mainframe software. Although it is somewhat tedious to calculate by hand, the procedure is fairly straightforward, provided one understands covariance algebra. For the difference between moderates and liberals, we have

$$\hat{V}(\hat{\tau}_2^P - \hat{\tau}_1^P) = \hat{V}(2\hat{\lambda}_{21}^{PC} - 2\hat{\lambda}_{11}^{PC})$$
$$= \hat{V}(2\hat{\lambda}_{21}^{PC}) + \hat{V}(2\hat{\lambda}_{11}^{PC}) - 2\hat{Cov}(2\hat{\lambda}_{21}^{PC}, 2\hat{\lambda}_{11}^{PC})$$
$$= 4[\hat{V}(\hat{\lambda}_{21}^{PC}) + \hat{V}(\hat{\lambda}_{11}^{PC}) - 2\hat{Cov}(\hat{\lambda}_{21}^{PC}, \hat{\lambda}_{11}^{PC})] .$$

The estimated variances and covariances of the lambdas are obtained from the variance-covariance matrix of parameter estimates shown in the bottom of Table A.1. Hence the estimated variance of the difference between the taus is 4 [(.00244) + (.00313) − 2(−.00129)] = .0326 (SPSS numbers the parameter estimates for easy reference). The estimated standard error is just the square root of this, or .181. Our test statistic for liberals versus moderates is then $z = [.098 - (-1.238)]/.181 = 7.38$. Because this is highly significant, we would conclude that moderates have significantly higher odds of voting for Bush. The other comparisons are made by testing the differences between the appropriate tau estimates.[3] The test for conservatives versus liberals is $z = [1.14 - (-1.238)]/.198 = 12.01$, while the comparison of conservatives versus moderates gives $z = (1.14 - .098)/.176 = 5.92$. These tests are both also highly significant.

In that we are performing multiple tests, we may want to employ the Bonferonni technique (Neter, Wasserman, & Kutner, 1985) to adjust for the resulting inflation in the Type I error rate. We determine the overall

Type I error rate that we wish to have apply to the total collection of comparisons. Typically, this will be .05. We then divide this by the total number of tests that we will make, which in this case is three. We get .05/3 = .0167. Each test is then made at an alpha of .0167. This ensures that the probability of making at least one Type I error over all three tests is no more than .0167 + .0167 + .0167 = .05. Even after making this adjustment for the tests above, we would conclude that the odds of voting for Bush are significantly different for each category of political views, such that the highest odds are for conservatives, the next highest odds are for moderates, and the lowest odds are for liberals.

Predictive Efficacy

The final issue to be considered in this chapter is the assessment of predictive efficacy for a given model. In logit modeling, predictive efficacy is to be distinguished from goodness of fit. The latter refers to the match between observed frequencies, on the one hand, and the frequencies one would see, on average, if the model in question were the true one that generated the data. Predictive efficacy, in contrast, refers to the ability of one's model to generate accurate predictions of a case's status on the dependent variable. It is quite possible to have an excellent fit between model and data without necessarily having a model with much predictive efficacy.

Consider any saturated model for a contingency table, for example. With a G^2 equal to zero, a saturated model always has a perfect fit to the data. Yet predictive efficacy is usually far from perfect. As long as there are some cases falling into each category of the dependent variable at any given combination of predictor values, a case's status on the dependent variable cannot be predicted with certainty from the model. In contrast, goodness of fit and predictive efficacy are treated as synonymous in linear regression. Both are typically assessed with the same statistic: R^2. Moreover, when a regression model is saturated, R^2 attains its maximum value of 1.

Magidson (1981) discusses two measures of predictive efficacy for logit models. Both are analogous to R^2 in that they describe the proportion of variation in the dependent variable that is accounted for by one's model. These are the concentration coefficient or CC (also known as Goodman and Kruskall's tau) and the uncertainty, or *entropy*, coefficient. The rationale and computation of the concentration coefficient will be discussed here; the reader is referred to Magidson (1981) or

TABLE 2.6

Calculation of Concentration Coefficient for the Logit Model of Vote Choice in Table 2.5

Political Views	Sex	Vote Choice Dukakis	Vote Choice Bush	n_{ij}^{PS}	Qualitative Variance SSE_v
Liberal	male	87.97	29.03	117	21.83
	female	109.03	35.97	145	27.05
Moderate	male	57.60	72.40	130	32.08
	female	90.40	113.60	204	50.34
Conservative	male	32.25	114.75	147	25.17
	female	35.75	127.25	163	27.91
Totals		413.00	493.00	906	184.38

Concentration coefficient = (224.73 − 184.38)/224.73 = .18.

Theil (1970) for a discussion of the uncertainty coefficient. The model of interest is the logit model of vote choice shown in Table 2.5.

The Concentration Coefficient. The expected frequencies from the model are reproduced in Table 2.6. These are in the columns labeled "Dukakis" and "Bush" (the other columns of the table will be discussed below). This model includes only the main effect of political views, and provides a good fit to the data, with a G^2 of 2.19 (df = 3, p = .53). The question is, how well does it account for vote choice?

To discuss the calculation of CC, let us use the following notation. Let the three-way table be such that there are i levels of political views, i = 1, 2, 3; j levels of sex, j = 1, 2; and k levels of vote choice, k = 1, 2. Further, let n = total sample size, n_1^C = the number of sample individuals voting for Dukakis, n_2^C = the number of sample individuals voting for Bush, n_{ij}^{PS} = the number of sample individuals in the ijth combination of political views and sex, $\hat{m}_{ij1}^{PSC}$ = the estimated expected frequency of voting for Dukakis (according to the model), among all those in the ijth combination of political views and sex, and $\hat{m}_{ij2}^{PSC}$ = the estimated expected frequency of voting for Bush, among all those in the ijth combination of political views and sex. The computations for the concentration coefficient are then as follows:

$$SSE_v = \sum_{ij} \frac{(\hat{m}_{ij1}^{PSC})(\hat{m}_{ij2}^{PSC})}{n_{ij}^{PS}},$$

$$SST_v = \frac{(n_1^C)(n_2^C)}{n},$$

$$CC = \frac{SST_v - SSE_v}{SST_v}.$$

The concentration coefficient is the percentage of qualitative variance accounted for by one's model. The quantity SST_v is the total variation in the qualitative dependent variable, vote choice. It is directly analogous to the total variation for a quantitative variable (Magidson, 1981). For the current problem, SST_v is (413)(493)/906 = 224.73.

In logit modeling SSE_v is the analogue of the residual sum of squares in regression. Each component that is summed in the formula for SSE_v above is the "residual" variation in vote choice at the ijth combination of political views and sex, according to the model. CC will range from 0 to 1, depending upon SSE_v. Under the model of complete independence between vote choice and the predictor set, the conditional distribution for vote choice at the ijth combination of political views and sex would be estimated to equal the marginal distribution for vote choice, for all i, j. In this case, SSE_v would be the same as SST_v, and CC would equal 0. If, on the other hand, a model were such that all individuals at the ijth combination of the predictors were estimated to vote for only one candidate, and this were true for all i, j, then each component of SSE_v in the formula would equal 0. The result is that SSE_v would equal 0, and CC would therefore equal 1.

The components of SSE_v for the logit model under investigation are shown in the column headed "Qualitative Variance" in Table 2.6. SSE_v is the sum of these components, and is shown to be 184.38 at the bottom of the column, in the "Totals" row. At the bottom of the table, the computations for CC result in a value of .18. The interpretation is that about 18% of the variation in vote choice is accounted for by the model. The concentration and entropy coefficients are both automatically printed by SPSS whenever logit models are requested.

3. LOGIT MODELS FOR MULTIDIMENSIONAL TABLES

The techniques discussed in Chapter 2 extend easily to tables of any number of dimensions. As the table becomes more complex, however, the number of possible models to consider increases exponentially.

Usually, under the guidance of theory, we are interested in estimating a particular model or, at most, a very small range of possible models. Yet there may be occasions when our research is more exploratory in nature and such theoretical guidance is lacking. Or we may find that a theoretically based model provides a poor fit to the data. It is often the discovery of a new pattern in the data that provides the impetus for the modification of theory or the generation of a new theory. Therefore, the researcher cannot afford to be insensitive to the discovery of unanticipated effects of this nature. This chapter will consider ways of exploring the data systematically to discover which associations are critical for achieving a good-fitting model. This is followed by a discussion of first-order interaction in logit models, and how odds ratios can be used to render these effects interpretable. I then expand the model to incorporate ordinal predictors, and indicate how the researcher can gauge whether incorporating information about category order is advantageous. The chapter concludes with a consideration of the problems introduced by small sample size.

Model Fitting

Let us examine the multidimensional contingency table of education by political views by vote choice by sex, shown in Table 3.1. This table has dimensions $H = 4$ (levels of education) by $I = 3$ (levels of political views) by $J = 2$ (levels of vote choice) by $K = 2$ (levels of sex), for a total of 48 cells. We are interested, once again, in estimating the log odds of voting for Bush, given education, political views, and sex. We will suppose, for the moment, that prior theory suggests that vote choice can be explained by a main effects model alone. That is, we expect the association between vote choice and each predictor to be constant over levels of the other two predictors.

When we fit the main effects logit model, SPE, SC, CP, CE (I will continue to represent logit models by listing the minimal sufficient marginals for the corresponding loglinear model) to the data, however, we find that it has a poor fit, with a G^2 of 38.27 (df = 17, p = .002). Hence one or more higher-order interaction terms are necessary in the model. The question is, which ones? In the absence of theoretical guidance, a systematic approach to model selection is required (see Benedetti & Brown, 1978, for an evaluation of the merits of various model selection strategies in loglinear modeling). Before illustrating this, however, I must first explain another type of chi-squared test used extensively in logit modeling: the *conditional* G^2 test.

TABLE 3.1
Four-Way Cross-Tabulation of Education, Political Views,
Vote Choice, and Sex

Education	Political Views	Choice	Sex Male	Sex Female
<12	liberal	Dukakis	12	15
		Bush	7	11
	moderate	Dukakis	9	17
		Bush	7	17
	conservative	Dukakis	6	11
		Bush	16	16
12	liberal	Dukakis	14	28
		Bush	7	12
	moderate	Dukakis	19	33
		Bush	21	48
	conservative	Dukakis	14	11
		Bush	27	48
13-15	liberal	Dukakis	17	32
		Bush	9	9
	moderate	Dukakis	19	24
		Bush	28	29
	conservative	Dukakis	3	11
		Bush	36	36
16+	liberal	Dukakis	46	33
		Bush	5	5
	moderate	Dukakis	11	16
		Bush	16	20
	conservative	Dukakis	4	8
		Bush	41	22

Conditional G^2 *Test.* Suppose that we have two models, which we will designate as Model A and Model B. Suppose, further, that Model A is composed of two sets of terms: set B and set B'. Model B, on the other hand, contains only set B. Hence in Model B all parameters contained in the set of terms B' have been set to zero. We say that Model B is *nested* within Model A, because all the terms in Model B are contained in Model A, but Model A has some additional terms (B') that are not contained in Model B. If Model A is a good-fitting model, then we can test whether the additional terms in Model A, that is, B', are necessary for fitting the data. The test is a conditional test for B', or a conditional test for Model B, given that Model A fits the data. Denoted

TABLE 3.2
Goodness-of-Fit Tests for Selected Logit Models of Table 3.1

Model	Terms in the Model	df	G^2	p
1	SPE, CPE, SCE, SCP	6	6.95	.3258
2	SPE, CPE, SCE	8	8.50	.3864
3	SPE, CPE, SC	11	14.49	.2072
4	SPE, SCE, CP	14	32.41	.0035
5	SPE, CPE	12	15.04	.2391
6	SPE, SC, CE, CP	17	38.27	.0023

by $G^2(B|A)$, the test is $G^2(B) - G^2(A)$. Under the null hypothesis that the parameters in B′ are all zero, this difference in chi-squared statistics is itself chi-squared, with df equal to the difference in df between Models A and B. If this conditional test is nonsignificant, then the set of terms B′ is not needed in the model. The set B′ can consist of one term or any number of terms. Moreover, this test can only be done using G^2 and not X^2. The reason for this is that if Model B is nested within Model A, then it will always be true that $G^2(B) \geq G^2(A)$. In other words, adding terms to a Model will never cause it to have a poorer fit to the observed data, as assessed by G^2 (just as adding terms to a linear regression model will never lower the unadjusted R^2). This property does not hold for the X^2 statistic (Bishop et al., 1975).

Table 3.2 presents goodness-of-fit tests (using G^2) for several logit models fitted to Table 3.1. (Table A.2 in the Appendix shows the BMDP program used to fit these models.) The G^2 value for each model can be used as a basis for making conditional tests, for example, G^2 for Model 1 containing all possible first-order interactions involving the dependent variable—denoted, in loglinear form, as SPE, CPE, SCE, SCP—is 6.95 (df = 6, p = .33). This model fits well, and contains nested within it the aforesaid main effects-only model denoted by SPE, SC, CP, CE. A conditional test for the three first-order interactions SCP, SCE, and CPE (SPE represents all possible associations among the predictors and must therefore be included in all models) is then $G^2(SPE, SC, CP, CE) - G^2(SPE, SCP, SCE, CPE) = 38.27 - 6.95 = 31.32$. With $17 - 6 = 11$ degrees of freedom, the test is highly significant ($p < .001$). Hence we must reject the null hypothesis that all parameters in these three interaction terms are simultaneously zero, and we should consider one or more of these terms for inclusion in the model. Do we need to consider inclusion of the second-order interaction term SCPE? No. The reason is that the goodness-of-fit test for Model 1 is at the same time a conditional test for the term SCPE. Adding SCPE to Model 1 results in the saturated model with a G^2 of zero and zero df. Hence G^2(Model 1|Saturated Model) = G^2(Model 1) − G^2(Saturated Model) = 6.95 − 0 = 6.95 with 6 − 0 = 6 df, a nonsignificant chi-squared value. Therefore, the SCPE term is not needed.

Using Model 1 as a base, we can then test whether the SCP term is needed in the model by performing the conditional G^2 test for Model 2—a model without SCP—given Model 1. The test is 8.50 − 6.95 = 1.55, with 2 df. As this result is not significant (p = .4607), we can drop SCP. Next, we test the SCE term with a conditional test for Model 3 given Model 2. The test is 14.49 − 8.50 = 5.99 with 3 df, a nonsignificant result (p = .1121). The SCE term can also be dropped. If, instead of testing SCE next, we had tested CPE by comparing Model 2 with Model 4, we would have obtained a conditional G^2 of 23.91 with 6 df. As this test is highly significant (p = .00054), CPE could not have been dropped. (Notice also that the same conclusion is reached by examining either model that excludes CPE—Models 4 and 6. Because neither model fits according to G^2, CPE is necessary for fitting the data.)

A conditional test for Model 6 given Model 3 tells us whether the last first-order interaction term, CPE, can be eliminated. Once again, the attempt to drop CPE results in a significant conditional G^2 of 23.78, with 6 df (p = .00057). It is clear that CPE—the first-order interaction between education and political ideology in their effects on vote choice—must be included in the model. In that only hierarchical models are of interest in this monograph,[4] retaining CPE automatically implies that the main effects of education and political views will also be retained. Therefore, the only term left to consider for deletion is the main effect of sex on vote choice, represented by SC. The appropriate test compares the G^2s for Models 3 and 5 and has a value of .55 with 1 df, which is not significant (p = .4583).

In logit notation, our final model (SPE, CPE) is

$$\log O_2^C = \alpha + \tau_h^E + \tau_i^P + \tau_{hi}^{EP}. \qquad [10]$$

In this model, "Bush" is once again category 2 of vote choice. Table 3.3 shows the parameter estimates for this model.

TABLE 3.3

Parameter Estimates for Logit Model (SPE, CPE) for Data
in Table 3.1

Effect		Additive Estimate	Multiplicative Estimate	Ratio to ASE
Intercept		.128	1.137	1.611
Polviews				
liberal		−1.194	.303	−10.191
moderate		.066	1.068	.628
conservative		1.130	3.096	9.858
EDUC				
<12		−.078	.925	−.544
12		.068	1.070	.552
13-15		.178	1.195	1.347
16+		−.168	.845	−1.142
EDUC * Polviews				
<12	liberal	.740	2.096	3.537
	moderate	−.194	.824	−.987
	conservative	−.546	.579	−2.639
12	liberal	.206	1.229	1.088
	moderate	.022	1.022	.134
	conservative	−.226	.798	−1.285
13-15	liberal	−.114	.892	−.583
	moderate	−.090	.914	−.527
	conservative	.202	1.224	1.031
16+	liberal	−.832	.435	−3.803
	moderate	.262	1.300	1.365
	conservative	.570	1.768	2.684

Interpretation of First-Order Interaction

In Chapter 2 we saw how, in a main-effects-only model, exponentiating
the difference between parameter estimates provided an estimate of the
odds ratio for individuals in one category of a predictor versus another.
When there is first-order interaction, however, the odds ratio for contrasting categories of a predictor is no longer invariant over levels of the other
predictors. Instead, it is a function of the levels of another predictor. In this
example, the ratio of the odds of voting for Bush, given contrasting
categories of political views, is dependent upon level of education. To see
this more clearly, let us first review interaction in linear regression.

Interaction in Regression. In the linear regression of a dependent variable, Y, on two predictors, X and Z, the interaction model is

$$E(Y) = \alpha + \beta_1 X + \beta_2 Z + \beta_3 XZ.$$

This equation can be rewritten to express the partial slope, or partial "effect" of X, as a function of Z:

$$E(Y) = \alpha + \beta_2 Z + (\beta_1 + \beta_3 Z)X.$$

In this form, the equation suggests that the partial effect of X on $E(Y)$ is dependent upon the level of Z. In fact, the partial slope for X, $\beta_1 + \beta_3 Z$, is composed of two terms: a constant, β_1, and an additive "correction," β_3, associated with a specific level of Z.

The Odds Ratio as the Partial "Effect." In the logit model, odds ratios represent the partial effects of predictors, and are therefore analogous to partial slopes in regression (this analogy will be even more complete when we discuss logit models with continuous predictors). If we express the odds ratio for conservatives versus liberals in terms of the parameters in Equation 10, we have

$$\frac{O_{23}^{CP}}{O_{21}^{CP}} = \frac{e^{\alpha} e^{\tau_h^{E}} e^{\tau_3^{P}} e^{\tau_{h3}^{EP}}}{e^{\alpha} e^{\tau_h^{E}} e^{\tau_1^{P}} e^{\tau_{h1}^{EP}}} = (e^{\tau_3^{P} - \tau_1^{P}})(e^{\tau_{h3}^{EP} - \tau_{h1}^{EP}}). \qquad [11]$$

Notice that the rightmost expression in Equation 11, representing the partial effect of political views on vote choice, is composed of two terms, much like the partial slope in the interactive regression model. The first of these terms is a constant $e^{\tau_3^{P} - \tau_1^{P}}$, while the second, $e^{\tau_{h3}^{EP} - \tau_{h1}^{EP}}$, is a multiplicative "correction" associated with a specific level of education. Hence the odds ratio for conservatives versus liberals depends upon level of education.

The interaction effect can be seen most clearly by recovering the odds ratios for each level of education. This is done by multiplying the constant in the rightmost expression in Equation 11 by the multiplicative correction for each level of education. From Table 3.3, the constant is exp[1.13 − (−1.194)] = 10.216. The corrections are as follows. For level 1 of education (< 12 years of schooling), we have exp[−.546 − (.740)] = .276; for level 2 (12 years of schooling), exp[−.226 − (.206)] = .649; for level 3 (13-15 years of schooling), exp[.202 − (−.114)] =

TABLE 3.4
Odds Ratios Depicting Interaction Between Education and Political Views in Their Effects on Vote Choice

A. *Odds Ratios for Contrasts of Political Views, by Education*

	Education			
Political Views Contrasts	*<12*	*12*	*13-15*	*16+*
Conservative vs. liberal	2.820	6.630	14.016	41.508
Moderate vs. liberal	1.385	2.933	3.610	10.526
Conservative vs. moderate	2.036	2.260	3.883	3.943

B. *Odds Ratios for Contrasts of Levels of Education, by Political Views*

	Political Views		
Education Contrasts	*Liberal*	*Moderate*	*Conservative*
12 vs. <12	.678	1.436	1.593
13-15 vs. <12	.550	1.434	2.730
16+ vs. <12	.190	1.442	2.790
13-15 vs. 12	.810	.998	1.712
16+ vs. 12	.280	1.004	1.751
16+ vs. 13-15	.346	1.007	1.023

1.372; and for level 4 (16 + years of schooling), exp[.570 − (−.832)] = 4.063. Apparently, lower levels of education reduce the odds ratio, while higher levels of education increase the odds ratio. When the constant is multiplied by each correction, the result is the odds ratio for conservatives versus liberals, for each level of education. These are displayed in the first row of panel A of Table 3.4.

The constant in the rightmost term of Equation 11 is actually the geometric mean of these four odds ratios. That is, 10.216 is equal to the fourth root of the product of the four odds ratios in the first row of panel A. In general, the constant term in the expression for the partial effect of a given predictor in the presence of first-order interaction is the geometric-mean odds ratio for the contrast between specific categories of that predictor (in this case conservatives versus liberals), across levels of the other variable. The constant is based on parameter estimates for the main effect of the first variable—in this case, political views. Therefore, the main effect of political views is the "average" effect across levels of education. The other two rows of panel A present, respectively, the odds ratios for moderates versus liberals, and conservatives versus moderates, as a function of education. These are recovered using expressions similar to Equation 11. For moderates versus liberals, the expression is

$$\frac{O_{22}^{CP}}{O_{21}^{CP}} = (e^{\tau_2^P - \tau_1^P})(e^{\tau_{h2}^{EP} - \tau_{h1}^{EP}}) .$$

Because only two of the three possible odds ratios are independent, the odds ratios for conservatives versus moderates are obtained simply by dividing the first row by the second.

Comparing the parameter estimates in Table 3.3 for the first-order interaction between education and political views with the odds ratios in panel A of Table 3.4 reveals why interpretations based on odds ratios are useful. The estimates for the category conservative are negative for the first two levels of education, while the estimates for the category liberal are positive. This gives the misleading impression that for those with 12 or fewer years of schooling, conservatives have lower odds of voting for Bush than liberals, while for those with more education, the reverse is the case. However, this effect is *relative* to what would be expected in the *absence of interaction*. Indeed, conservatives have *higher* odds of voting for Bush than liberals regardless of level of education, as shown by the odds ratios in the first column in panel A of Table 3.4. This difference becomes more pronounced, however, as education increases, suggesting an interaction effect that is ordinal in nature.

The interaction can also be viewed as the effect of education on vote choice, as a function of political views. That is, we can estimate the odds ratios for contrasts between levels of education separately for each category of political views. For example, the odds ratio for those with 16 or more years of schooling (level 4 of education) versus those with fewer than 12 years of schooling (level 1 of education) is seen to be a function of political views:

$$\frac{O_{24}^{CE}}{O_{21}^{CE}} = \frac{e^\alpha e^{\tau_4^E} e^{\tau_i^P} e^{\tau_{4i}^{EP}}}{e^\alpha e^{\tau_1^E} e^{\tau_i^P} e^{\tau_{1i}^{EP}}} = (e^{\tau_4^E - \tau_1^E})(e^{\tau_{4i}^{EP} - \tau_{1i}^{EP}}) . \qquad [12]$$

Substituting the appropriate parameter estimates from Table 3.3 into the rightmost expression in Equation 12, we arrive at odds ratios for those with 16 or more, versus 12 or fewer, years of schooling of .19 for liberals, 1.442 for moderates, and 2.79 for conservatives. Panel B of Table 3.4 shows these as well as all other odds ratios formed by contrasting pairs of levels of education. These ratios are listed separately by categories of political views.

Examined from this perspective, the interaction is disordinal. The odds ratios reveal that, among liberals, having a higher level of education is associated with lower odds of voting for Bush, for each contrast involving a higher versus a lower level of education. As political views change from liberal to moderate to conservative, however, these odds ratios systematically increase. Among conservatives, having a higher level of education is associated with considerably higher odds of voting for Bush. Moreover, because the interaction is disordinal, the main effect of education tends to "wash out" when averaged over categories of political views. Parameter estimates in Table 3.3 for the main effects of education reveal a somewhat curvilinear pattern in the logits with increasing education, but none of these effects is significant. In contrast, the main effect of political views is still significant even after averaging over levels of education.

Further inspection of the odds ratios in Table 3.4 reveals several monotonic trends that can be exploited by treating both education and political views as ordinal variables. In particular, we notice that all comparisons in panel A involving those who are more, rather than less, conservative result in odds ratios greater than unity. Thus the odds of voting for Bush appear to increase in a monotonic fashion as political views change from liberal to moderate to conservative. Additionally, each of these odds ratios increases in a monotonic fashion with increasing education. Similarly, the odds ratios in panel B increase in a monotonic fashion as political views change from liberal to moderate to conservative. Let us now consider how ordinal predictors can be incorporated into the logit model.

Modeling Ordinal Predictors

When there appears to be a linear relationship between the logit and the categories of an ordinal variable, as in the vote choice example above, it is advantageous to exploit this trend. For example, the main effects-only model of vote choice as a function of education and political views, with both predictors treated as ordinal, is

$$\log O_{\text{BUSH}}^{\text{C}} = \alpha + \beta^{\text{E}}(e_h) + \beta^{\text{P}}(p_i), \qquad [13]$$

where $e_h = h$, for $h = 1, \ldots, 4$ and $p_i = i$ for $i = 1, \ldots, 3$. That is, e_h and p_i are simply the integers representing the levels of education and political views, respectively. The parameters β^E and β^P represent the increment to the log odds of voting for Bush brought about by a one-unit increase in the levels of education and political views, respectively.

Let us compare Equation 13 to the corresponding logit model that treats both predictors as nominal:

$$\log O_{\text{BUSH}}^C = \alpha + \tau_h^E + \tau_i^P . \qquad [14]$$

Equation 13 imposes a linear structure on the tau parameters for education and political views; that is, $\tau_h^E = \beta^E(e_h)$ and $\tau_i^P = \beta^P(p_i)$. Moreover, Equation 13 requires 3 fewer parameters than Equation 14—only 1 parameter is estimated for each predictor, compared with 3 for education and 2 for political views in Equation 14. Therefore, Equation 13 is nested inside Equation 14.[5] Because of this nesting property, were Equation 14 a good-fitting model, we could test whether the additional parameters in Equation 14, compared with Equation 13, were necessary for fitting the data. This would, in effect, be a test of the null hypothesis that the logit is linearly related to the predictors, or a test for linearity. The test would be $G^2(13) - G^2(14)$. If this test were nonsignificant, then such a linear model would be acceptable. However, the test is not valid because, as we saw earlier, Equation 14 does not fit well; nor does 13, with a $G^2 = 42.24$, df $= 21, p = .004$.

The problem, of course, is that there is a significant interaction between education and political views in their effects on the logit of vote choice. Further, because of the linearity in the interaction, as discussed above, we need simply add one more parameter to Equation 13 to fit the data—a cross-product term representing the first-order interaction:

$$\log O_{\text{BUSH}}^C = \alpha + \beta^E(e_h) + \beta^P(p_i) + \beta^{EP}(e_h p_i) . \qquad [15]$$

This model has a very good fit to Table 3.1, with a $G^2 = 20.2$, df $= 20$, $p = .45$. Moreover, because Equation 15 is nested inside Equation 10—with the interaction term taking the structured form $\tau_{hi}^{EP} = \beta^{EP}(e_h p_i)$— a test for linearity can be conducted by taking $G^2(15) - G^2(10) = 20.2 - 15.04 = 5.16$, with $20 - 12 = 8$ df. This tests the null hypothesis, H_0: $\{\tau_h^E = \beta^E(e_h)\}$, $\{\tau_i^P = \beta^P(p_i)\}$, $\{\tau_{hi}^{EP} = \beta^{EP}(e_h p_i)\}$, against the alternative that at least one of the taus is not a linear function of e_h, p_i, or their cross product. In that this conditional test is very nonsignificant ($p > .25$), we conclude that the assumption of linearity in the relationship between

TABLE 3.5
Parameter Estimates for Logit Models 13 and 15

| Effect | No-Interaction Model | | Interaction Model | |
	Additive Estimate	Ratio to ASE	Additive Estimate	Ratio to ASE
Intercept	−2.176	—	.066	—
Education	−.019	−.265	−.890	−4.383
Political views	1.186	11.946	.050	.194
Education * political views	—	—	.446	4.602
G^2	42.240	—	20.200	—
df	21.000	—	20.000	—
p	.004	—	.450	—

the logit of vote choice and both predictors is reasonable. Freeing the linearity constraint by employing Equation 10 results in no significant improvement in fit.

Notice, also, that we have gained 8 df for test of the model by treating both predictors as ordinal. In general, when the relationship between the logit and a given variable with ordered categories is indeed linear, we gain power for testing the significance of that relationship by modeling that variable as ordinal. However, should the relationship be nonlinear, we will actually lose power for detecting departures from independence. This is due to the fact that models such as 13 and 15 are designed to capitalize upon linear structure in modeling dependence. But this is at the sacrifice of power for detecting types of dependence that are not so structured (Agresti, 1990). When the logit is related to an ordered categorical variable in a nonlinear fashion, we are better advised to treat that variable as qualitative.

Table 3.5 shows the resulting parameter estimates for fitting both Equations 13 and 15 to Table 3.1 (the associated SPSS program is given in Table A.3 in the Appendix). The estimates for Equation 13 appear under the heading "No-Interaction Model," while those for 15 appear under the heading "Interaction Model." Equation 13 suggests that, controlling for education, each unit increase in level of political views— for example, an increase from liberal to moderate or from moderate to conservative—increases the odds of voting for Bush by a factor of exp(1.186) = 3.274. Each unit increase in education, on the other hand, is estimated to reduce the odds of voting for Bush: The multiplicative impact is exp(−.019) = .981. This model, however, fits poorly.

The interaction model shows why. There is a substantial and significant interaction effect: The z test for β^{EP} is 4.602. The interaction can be seen either by considering the partial effect of political views on vote choice, expressed as a function of education, or by considering the partial effect of education on vote choice, expressed as a function of political views. From the first perspective, we write the model as

$$\log O^C_{BUSH} = 0.066 - 0.890\,(e_h) + [0.05 + 0.446\,(e_h)](p_i)\,.$$

This way of expressing Equation 15 shows that the partial effect of political views depends upon level of education. In particular, each higher level of education increases the partial effect of political views by .446. For example, the partial effect of a unit increase in political views on the log odds of voting for Bush is .05 + .446 = .496 for those with fewer than 12 years (level 1) of education, .05 + .446(2) = .942 for those with 12 years (level 2) of education, and so forth. Thus, for those with fewer than 12 years of education, each unit increase in political views increases the odds of voting for Bush by a factor of exp(.496) = 1.642. For those with 16 or more years of education, however, each unit increase in political views increases the odds by exp[.05 + .446(4)] = 6.259. The ordinal nature of the interaction is evident, in that the log odds increases in a linear fashion with an increase in the level of political views, regardless of education.

By recombining terms in Equation 15, we arrive at the other perspective on the interaction:

$$\log O^C_{BUSH} = 0.066 + [-0.890 + 0.446\,(p_i)](e_h) + 0.05\,(p_i)\,.$$

Now it can be seen that, for "low levels" of conservatism—that is, for liberals—the partial effect of education is to reduce the odds of voting for Bush: the multiplicative impact of each unit increase in education is exp[-.890 + .446(1)] = .641. In contrast, for conservatives, the partial effect of education is to increase the odds of voting for Bush: the multiplicative impact of each unit increase in education now becomes exp[-.890 + .446(3)] = 1.565. Clearly, when viewed from this perspective, the interaction is disordinal.

These results agree with the trends shown in Table 3.4. There, although both predictors were treated as qualitative, the linearity in the relationships between the odds ratios and the levels of education and political views was quite evident. Exploiting these linearities by treating the predictors as ordinal provides parameter estimates that summarize these patterns in a compact and elegant fashion.

Sample Size Considerations

Statistical inference in logit modeling rests largely upon the asymptotic behavior of sample statistics—behavior that obtains as the sample size increases toward infinity. In order for these asymptotic properties to be approximately valid, the sample must be relatively large. A rule of thumb is that average cell size (sample size divided by number of cells) should be at least 5. Tables with average cell sizes smaller than this are referred to as "sparse" tables. Even in sparse tables, however, if only a limited number of possible models is being investigated, the researcher can still be on safe ground with inferential tests (Fienberg, 1980). One check for whether sample size is a problem in sparse tables is to compare the substantive conclusions reached using G^2, as opposed to X^2, in testing model fit. If the conclusions are not the same, then the sample is too small to make valid judgments (Agresti, 1990; Clogg & Eliason, 1988). Short of collecting more observations, one solution is to collapse the table over one or more variables. Agresti (1990) gives conditions under which tables may be safely collapsed without changing relationships among key variables.

Empty Cells. A problem that is often related to sample size is the occurrence of empty, or *zero*, cells. Actually, zero cells are of two types. Structural zeros have nothing to do with sample size. They arise because certain cross-classifications of the variables cannot logically occur. For example, in a study of sex differences in the existence of complications following different types of surgery, any cells arising from the cross-classifications "male, hysterectomy" and "female, prostatectomy" would logically be empty. The solution to this problem is to form a logit model for the part of the table containing nonzero cells, and proceed with the analysis. Examples are found in Agresti (1990) and Bishop et al. (1975).

Sampling zeros arise much more frequently, and simply reflect the fact that the sample is not large enough to provide nonzero observations for certain cross-classifications that occur with low frequency in the population. Degrees of freedom for test of a model may be adversely affected by these types of cells, depending upon how they are arrayed in the table. Both BMDP and SPSS automatically adjust for sampling zeros in calculating degrees of freedom. A remedy for any difficulties caused by sampling zeros is to add a small constant to each cell in the table prior to analysis. Guidelines for finding the appropriate constant to add to each cell are given by Clogg and Eliason (1988).

Summary of Model Assumptions. Up to this point, I have been concerned with the development and explication of logit models for contingency-table data. Before moving on to consider models for disaggregated, or individual-level, data, let me briefly summarize the assumptions required for the analysis of contingency tables using logit techniques. First, the dependent variable is assumed to be dichotomous (this restriction will be relaxed, however, in Chapter 5, where I will explain how to model a polytomous response). Second, the data are assumed to have been collected under one of the three sampling schemes outlined in Chapter 2. Third, individual observations are assumed to be independent of one another. Fourth, predictors are not continuous, and are assumed to have a finite—and typically small—number of levels. Fifth, either the predictors are fixed by design or it is acceptable to treat them as fixed. That is, the categories or levels manifested by the predictors are exactly those that are of interest, and do not simply represent a random sample from a larger "population" of levels of interest. The implication is that these values would remain the same over repeated sampling from the population of individuals that generated the current sample. Finally, the sample size is "large" by the criteria developed in the previous section.

4. LOGISTIC REGRESSION

The preceding chapters have examined logit modeling for data in multidimensional contingency tables. When continuous explanatory variables are employed, however, the contingency-table format is appropriate only with replicated data—that is, data in which there are several cases having the same combinations of levels of the predictors. More often, this condition is not met. Therefore, logit modeling with continuous predictors is accomplished with disaggregated, or individual-level, data, much as in linear regression. Accordingly, the technique is referred to as *logistic regression.* (Another commonly used technique that is based on somewhat different assumptions is *probit* analysis, discussed in Aldrich & Nelson, 1984; Hanushek & Jackson, 1977.) In this chapter I develop the logistic regression model, give its assumptions, and show its similarity to the models of the previous chapter. I also show how to explore potential nonlinearity in the relationship between the logit and a continuous predictor, controlling for other predictors in the model. I show, once again, how to model interaction, how to test for sets of terms in the model, and how to assess predictive efficacy. The final section of this chapter shows how logistic regression can be used to evaluate whether a set of intervening variables accounts for the impact of one or more explanatory variables on the response.

Logistic Regression for a Binary Response

I have compiled a set of data for a random sample of 54 U.S. standard metropolitan statistical areas (SMSAs). The response variable of interest is the murder rate in 1980, recorded as the number of homicides per 100,000 population. For didactic purposes I have recoded this as a dichotomous response, based upon splitting this variable at its median of 6.1 for the 54 cities. The resulting binary variable, Murder Rate, is coded simply as "low" or "high." Because it results in loss of information, collapsing an interval-level variable for the purpose of performing a logistic regression is not, in general, a recommended procedure. Nevertheless, many dichotomous observed variables are only proxies for underlying interval-level variables that measurement inadequacy prevents us from observing precisely (Hagle & Mitchell, in press; McKelvey & Zavoina, 1975). Therefore, it can be instructive to develop logistic regression with such an artificial response so that results can be compared with an OLS regression on the "underlying" continuous variable.

The three explanatory variables are all continuous: 1980 Population Size in thousands, Percentage Change in Population Size from 1970 to 1980, and the Reading Quotient, a rough measure of literacy. The latter is obtained by adding the total number of library volumes in a city to the total number of volumes checked out annually, and dividing the result by the population size (Boyer & Savageau, 1981). A high rate of growth is associated with an increase in population density and social crowding. Both of these conditions are likely to increase social stress, which, in turn, may result in an increase in violent crime. Greater literacy may be associated with a higher educational level in a given

SMSA, which may in turn be related to a lower incidence of homicide. We will see whether the results support these predictions.

Any particular combination of observed predictor values is referred to as a *covariate pattern* (Hosmer & Lemeshow, 1989). In this set of data, no pattern is replicated; hence a cross-tabulation of cases by all four variables would result in a contingency table in which half of the cells would be empty and the other half would contain only one observation each. This situation arises because continuous variables can take on any value in the real numbers, resulting in unique covariate patterns for each case. A consequence is that G^2 and X^2 can no longer be assumed to have asymptotic chi-squared distributions. These statistics converge in distribution to chi-squared only under the assumption that the total number of cells is fixed while the sample size is increased to infinity. With continuous predictors, it is not realistic to assume that the number of cells remains fixed as sample size increases, because each new case potentially adds a new cell to the table. Therefore, as sample size increases, so does the number of cells. We get around this problem by taking a different approach to model estimation, as explained below.

The Model

Let P_i = 1980 Population Size in thousands; C_i = Growth Rate—indexed by Percentage Change in Population from 1970 to 1980; and R_i = Reading Quotient, for the ith SMSA, where $i = 1, 2, \ldots, 54$. Further, let π_i = the conditional probability that the Murder Rate for the ith SMSA is high, and $1 - \pi_i$ the conditional probability that it is low, given P_i, C_i, and R_i. Then the logistic regression model for the log odds of a high murder rate is

$$\log \frac{\pi_i}{1 - \pi_i} = \log O_i = \alpha + \beta_1(P_i) + \beta_2(C_i) + \beta_3(R_i) , \qquad [16]$$

where O_i is simply the conditional odds of having a high murder rate, given the explanatory variables. Notice that Equation 16 is very similar to Equation 13, except that it models each ith observation separately, and that the units in which the predictors are measured represent precise quantities. Therefore, there is very little change in model form as we proceed from contingency-table to disaggregated data. The betas represent the change in the log odds due to unit increments in the values of the predictors. The multiplicative version of Equation 16 is obtained, as before, by exponentiating both sides of the equation:

$$O_i = e^{\alpha} e^{\beta_1 (P_i)} e^{\beta_2 (C_i)} e^{\beta_3 (R_i)} . \qquad [17]$$

Here the analogy between odds ratios and partial linear regression coefficients is complete. $\text{Exp}(\beta_1)$ is the odds ratio for SMSAs that are a unit (1,000 inhabitants) apart on population size, controlling for the Growth Rate and the Reading Quotient. Similar interpretations apply to the other beta coefficients.

Estimation Via Maximum Likelihood

In the contingency-table case, we found the MLEs of the expected frequencies by "fitting" the minimal sufficient marginals for a given model. Parameter estimates were then recovered by substituting the MLEs of the expected frequencies into the definitional formulas for the parameters. In logistic regression, we estimate the parameters directly, again using maximum likelihood. As before, it is necessary to know the probability distribution for the observed data. In particular, it is necessary to know the conditional distribution of the dependent variable, given each covariate pattern, expressed in terms of the parameters. Because the dependent variable is dichotomous, this distribution is readily obtained.

If we represent the dependent variable for the ith SMSA as a dummy variable, Y_i, such that $Y_i = 1$ if the murder rate is high, and $Y_i = 0$ if it is low, then Y_i has the Bernoulli distribution at each covariate pattern, with mean $= \pi_i$ and variance $= \pi_i (1 - \pi_i)$. To specify this distribution further as a function of alpha and the betas, we must also assume that the relationship between π_i and the predictors takes on a specific functional form. Here, we assume that form to be the logistic distribution function,[6] just as, in regression, we assume that the mean of Y is related to the predictors through a linear function. As in regression, our choice of functional form appears to fit real-world data quite well, most of the time. That is, in practice, the logistic distribution function is often a good model for the π_i, the conditional probabilities of event occurrence. (An alternative distribution function is the standard normal; this leads to probit analysis.) A theoretical rationale for using the logistic curve can be found in Aldrich and Nelson (1984).

Estimation proceeds by finding estimates for alpha and the betas that maximize the resulting conditional distribution, or likelihood, function for the set of sample values $y_1, y_2, \ldots, y_n$.[7] This results in values for the parameters that would have made the sample data most likely to have been observed. For large samples, the parameter estimates tend to follow a normal distribution; therefore, estimates divided by their estimated asymptotic standard errors provide z tests for the significance of coefficients.

Logistic Regression for Cities Data

The estimated coefficients (estimated asymptotic standard errors for sample betas in parentheses) for Equation 16 are (Table A.4 in the Appendix shows the SAS program that produced these estimates, with MURDRATE as the binary dependent variable):

$$\log \hat{O}_i = 1.1387 + 0.0014(P_i) + 0.0561(C_i) - 0.4050(R_i) .$$
$$\quad\quad\quad (0.0009) \quad\quad (0.0227) \quad\quad (0.1568)$$

Of the three predictors, only the growth rate and the reading quotient have significant effects on the odds of a high murder rate ($p = .0136$ and .0098, respectively). As expected, dichotomizing the dependent variable has resulted in a loss of information and a concomitant loss of statistical power. The OLS results (using the continuous murder rate) agree substantively with the logistic regression results, but find all three coefficients highly significant ($p < .005$ for all three predictors).

The interpretations of logistic regression coefficients are as follows. Let b_j represent the sample estimate of β_j, the coefficient for the jth predictor. Then b_j estimates the change in the *log odds* of being in the category of interest on the response for a one-unit increase in the jth predictor, controlling for all other predictors in the model. Moreover, $\exp(b_j)$ is the estimated multiplicative change in the *odds* for a one-unit increase in the jth predictor, and $100[\exp(b_j) - 1]$ is the estimated *percentage* change in the *odds* for a one-unit increase in the jth predictor. In the current example, each additional percentage that the population increased is estimated to increase the odds of having a high murder rate by a factor of $\exp(.0561) = 1.058$, or about $100(1.058 - 1) = 5.8\%$. Each unit increase in the reading quotient, on the other hand, *reduces* the odds of having a high murder rate by a factor of $\exp(-.4050) = .667$, or eventuates in a $100(.667 - 1) = -33.3\%$ change (i.e., in a 33.3% *reduction*) in the odds of a high murder rate.

Global Test for the Predictor Set. In linear regression the global F test is used to test the null hypothesis that all regression coefficients in the model are simultaneously zero in the population. If this hypothesis is rejected, it can be concluded that at least one beta is nonzero, and individual t tests for these betas can reveal which of them are nonzero. From the OLS results (using the continuous murder rate), F is 12.1 with 3 and 50 degrees of freedom, a highly significant result ($p < .0001$).

In logistic regression, the analogue of the global F test is a likelihood-ratio chi-squared test statistic, which is often referred to as the model chi-squared. We test H_0, all of the betas in Equation 16 equal zero, against H_1, at least one beta is not zero. The test is based on evaluating the likelihood function for the Y_i at the MLEs under each hypothesis. Under the null hypothesis, the only parameter in the model is α, and the likelihood function evaluated at the MLE for α is denoted L_0. The likelihood function evaluated under H_1, denoted L_1, is the function evaluated at the MLEs for all of the parameters in the model. The model chi-squared statistic is then $-2 \log(L_0) - [-2 \log(L_1)]$, which, if the null hypothesis is true, has the chi-squared distribution with df equal to the number of parameters in the model, not counting the intercept (Hosmer & Lemeshow, 1989). This test statistic is $74.860 - 54.635 = 20.225$, which, with 3 df, is also highly significant ($p = .0002$). Therefore, we can conclude that at least one of the betas in Equation 16 is nonzero, and, as already noted, z tests (parameter estimate divided by its asymptotic standard error) suggest that both β_2 and β_3 are the nonzero coefficients.

It should be emphasized that the model chi-squared test is quite different from G^2, the goodness-of-fit measure used in contingency-table analyses. Whereas G^2 assesses the fit of the model to the data, the model chi-squared in logistic regression tests only whether any of the predictors are linearly related to the log odds of the event of interest. It is *not* a test for the goodness of fit of the model to the data. Such a test is, however, available in BMDP, and is automatically provided as part of the output from its Stepwise Logistic Regression program. It is calculated by grouping all of the covariate patterns in the data into 10 categories, based upon deciles of the model-generated predicted probabilities of event occurrence. This statistic has a chi-squared distribution with 8 degrees of freedom under the null hypothesis that the model is correct (Hosmer & Lemeshow, 1989). Nevertheless, it is my experience that this test tends to confirm almost any model, and is therefore not as useful as measures of predictive efficacy, to be discussed at the end of this chapter.

Obtaining Predicted Probabilities. Although my emphasis throughout this monograph has been on the interpretation of results in terms of odds and odds ratios, there may be interest in obtaining predicted probabilities of event occurrence, based on the model. These are readily obtained from the predicted odds or log odds. In general, if $\hat{O}_i$ is the estimated conditional odds of event occurrence, based on the estimated logistic regression equation, then it is easy to see that the estimated probability of event occurrence, given a specific covariate pattern, is

$$\frac{\hat{O}_i}{1+\hat{O}_i} = \left(\frac{\hat{\pi}_i}{1-\hat{\pi}_i}\right) \Bigg/ \left(1+\frac{\hat{\pi}_i}{1-\hat{\pi}_i}\right) = \hat{\pi}_i.$$

To illustrate, the estimated odds of having a high murder rate for a city having a 1980 population size of 200,000, a growth rate of 12% between 1970 and 1980, and a reading quotient of 10 is, using Equation 17,

$$\hat{O}_i \mid 200, 12, 10 = e^{1.1387} e^{0.0014(200)} e^{0.0561(12)} e^{-0.405(10)}$$

$$= (3.123)(1.0014)^{200}(1.058)^{12}(0.667)^{10} = 0.142. \quad [18]$$

The estimated probability of having a high murder rate for this city is then .142/(1 + .142) = .124. This method of calculating conditional probabilities from conditional odds is applicable not only to the logistic regression model, but to any of the logit models discussed in previous chapters as well.

Odds Versus Probabilities. Interpreting logistic regression results in terms of odds rather than probabilities confers certain advantages. Most important among these is that $\exp(\beta)$ is a single summary statistic for the partial effect of a given predictor on the odds, controlling for other predictors in the model. There is no comparable statistic for the probability. That is, it is not possible to summarize the impact on the conditional probability of a unit increase in a given predictor, net of the others. The reason for this is that the model is nonlinear, and therefore nonadditive, in the probabilities. When Equation 16 is written in terms of the conditional probability, π_i, of having a high murder rate, for the ith SMSA, we have

$$\pi_i = \frac{\exp\left[\alpha + \beta_1(P_i) + \beta_2(C_i) + \beta_3(R_i)\right]}{1 + \exp\left[\alpha + \beta_1(P_i) + \beta_2(C_i) + \beta_3(R_i)\right]}. \quad [19]$$

The right-hand side of this equation is, of course, the logistic distribution function, which describes a complex nonlinear surface in four dimensions. The partial effect on π_i of a given predictor, say, the reading quotient, net of all other predictors, is given by $\beta_3(\pi_i)(1 - \pi_i)$. Because π_i is a function of the values of all explanatory variables in the model, this partial "slope" depends upon the specific covariate pattern at which it is evaluated. Therefore, in contrast to partial slopes in linear regression, the partial slope for the effect of a given predictor on the probability is not a constant (for an expanded discussion of this issue, see DeMaris, 1990).

Modeling Nonlinearity. Until now it has been assumed that the relationship between a given predictor and the logit will be linear, controlling for other effects. This may not be a safe assumption, however. Nonlinear relationships between the logit and a given predictor may be quite pronounced in the data, but will not be detected unless this assumption is examined. Fortunately, it is a simple matter to check for linearity in a given predictor. One such procedure involves grouping the continuous predictor into several categories, based on quartiles or quintiles of its distribution. These categories are then represented by dummy variables (one fewer dummy than the number of categories), with the lowest group as the reference category. The dummies are then substituted into the logistic regression equation in place of the continuous predictor, and the model is reestimated. The estimates for the dummies can then be plotted against the midpoints of the grouped categories. If the logit is linear in the predictor, the resulting plotted points will fall on a straight line. Departures from a straight line reveal the extent of nonlinearity in this relationship (Hosmer & Lemeshow, 1989).

I will illustrate this procedure for the predictor Growth Rate in Equation 16. The range of this variable was −3.8 to 68. Grouping based on quintiles of the distribution produced categories with midpoints at −.37, 6.64, 15.05, 23.27, and 47.9, with approximately a fifth of the cities falling into each category. Model 1 in Table 4.1 shows the result of estimating a logistic regression for the log odds of a high murder rate using 1980 Population Size, Reading Quotient, and the four dummies representing the second through the fifth quintiles of Growth Rate (labeled "Quintile 2-Quintile 5").

From an examination of the dummy coefficients, it is clear that the logit increases monotonically from Quintile 2 through Quintile 5. But is the increase linear? A plot of the dummy coefficients against the category midpoints, shown in Figure 4.1, helps to resolve the question.

TABLE 4.1

Logistic Regression Results From Estimating Various Models for the
Log Odds of a High Murder Rate, for 54 SMSAs

| Effect | Model 1 | Parameter Estimates | | |
		Model 2	Model 3	Model 4
Intercept	.1562	.3501	1.0304	1.4487
Quintile 2	1.2707	—	—	—
Quintile 3	1.6705	—	—	—
Quintile 4	2.1396	—	—	—
Quintile 5	2.7236*	—	—	—
Growth Rate (%)	—	.1266*	.0176	.0346
Growth^2	—	−.0013	—	—
Growth * Population	—	—	.0001	—
1980 Population	.0016	.0016	.0004	.0016
Reading Quotient	−.3556*	−.3780*	−.3369*	−.4818*
Eastern SMSA	—	—	—	−.0012
Western SMSA	—	—	—	1.5166

*$p < .05$.

While it is sufficient to plot the four dummies against their category midpoints, I have instead plotted the estimated logits for all five categories of Growth Rate against all five midpoints. These logits are obtained by successively adding each dummy coefficient to the intercept, with the intercept itself representing the estimated logit for the first quintile. Specifically, the first point is (−.37, .1562), the second point is (6.64, .1562 + 1.2707), the third point is (15.05, .1562 + 1.6705), and so on. The resulting plot represents the trend in the logit with each successive quintile, and includes the point representing the first quintile. Moreover, the plot shows the trend in the logit from Quintile 1 through Quintile 5 at constant values of the other predictors. The effect of evaluating Model 1 at fixed values of the other predictors will simply be to shift the plot up or down by a constant.

The plot suggests that the relationship is a curvilinear one, in which an increase in the Growth Rate has a declining impact on the logit, from the first through the fifth quintiles. A quadratic term can be used to capture this trend effectively. Model 2 shows the result of adding Growth-squared ("Growth^2" in the table) to Equation 16. While the main effect for Growth Rate is positive, the coefficient for Growth^2 is negative. To see more clearly how these coefficients describe the curve,

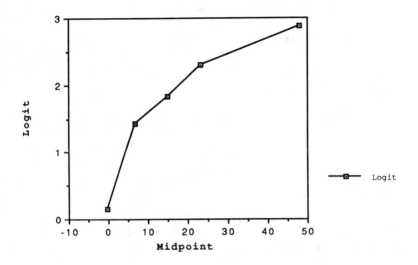

Figure 4.1. Logits Plotted Against Midpoints of Grouped Levels of Population Growth

we write the estimated equation so that the partial slope for Growth Rate is expressly seen to be a function of the level of Growth Rate:

$$\log \hat{O}_i = 0.3501 + [0.1266 - 0.0013(C_i)](C_i) + 0.0016(P_i) - 0.378(R_i).$$

The partial slope is composed of two terms: a constant, .1266, plus an additive correction for level of Growth Rate, $-.0013(C_i)$. Therefore, each percentage increase in Growth Rate decreases the partial slope by .0013. While the partial slope is positive throughout, it is higher at low levels of Growth. In practice we would probably not retain the quadratic term in the model, as it is nonsignificant. In that the linear component of the partial slope is significant, Equation 16 represents the more parsimonious model for the data.

Modeling Interaction. As in the logit model with ordinal predictors, the interaction of two continuous predictors in their effects on the logit is modeled using a cross-product term. We might speculate, for example, that rapid growth has more deleterious effects for small cities than for large ones. Small communities are more likely to change radically in character with rapid growth, compared with larger cities. We can test this by taking the product of Growth Rate with Population Size and including it in Equation 16. Model 3 in Table 4.1 shows the result (Growth * Population is the interaction term). Expressing the partial slope for Growth Rate as a function of Population Size reveals the character of the interaction:

$$\log \hat{O_i} = 1.0304 + 0.0004 (P_i) + [0.0176 + 0.0001 (P_i)](C_i) - 0.3369 (R_i),$$

The partial slope for the effect of Growth Rate is $[.0176 + .0001(P_i)]$. The result is opposite to the hypothesis. Each unit increase in population—that is, each additional 1,000 people—increases the partial slope for Growth Rate by .0001. Hence growth has a stronger impact on the log odds of a high murder rate in larger SMSAs than it does in smaller ones. However, the illustration again is purely didactic; the interaction effect is not significant.

Testing Subsets of Coefficients. While individual z tests can determine the significance of individual parameters, there are times when it is of interest to test several parameters simultaneously. One may, for example, desire to test whether a subset of explanatory variables is significantly related to the logit once other variables have been included in the model. Or, if a given predictor is categorical with M categories, a test for the impact of that predictor is a test of the null hypothesis that all $M - 1$ dummies representing that variable are zero. In either case, ΔC^2, the difference in model chi-squareds for models with and without the parameters in question, is itself a chi-squared test of the null hypothesis, with df equal to the number of parameters being tested. If ΔC^2 is significant, then at least one of these parameters is nonzero.

As an example, Model 4 in Table 4.1 shows the results of adding two dummy variables representing region to the model containing 1980 Population, Growth Rate, and Reading Quotient. "Eastern SMSA" is a dummy variable representing eastern cities, and "Western SMSA" is a dummy for western cities. The contrast category is midwestern cities. The model chi-squared for this model is 22.856. Earlier we found that the model chi-squared without the region dummies was 20.225. A test for whether region of the country is significant is then $22.856 - 20.225 = 2.631$. With 2 df, this is very nonsignificant. Apparently, region as conceptualized here is not a significant predictor of high murder rates.

Interpreting Dummy Coefficients. Dummy coefficients represent the increment to the logit associated with specific categories of a qualitative variable. In particular, if one exponentiates a dummy coefficient, one recovers the estimated odds ratio for those in the category of interest versus those in the contrast category. For example, the estimated ratio of the odds of having a high murder rate for western, versus midwestern, cities is $\exp(1.5166) = 4.557$. The odds ratio for eastern, versus midwestern, cities is estimated as $\exp(-.0012) = .999$. The last odds ratio—for eastern, versus western, cities—is estimated as $\exp[-.0012 - (1.5166)] = .219$. None of these ratios, however, is significantly different from one.

Predictive Efficacy in Logistic Regression

Several measures have been proposed for assessing predictive efficacy in logistic regression. Here I shall discuss three. All are easily obtained from standard logistic regression output.

A Measure Based on the Log Likelihood. Recall that the model chi-squared in logistic regression is equal to $-2 \log(L_0) - [-2 \log(L_1)]$, with degrees of freedom equal to the number of parameters—other than the intercept—in the model. It turns out that, in linear regression, under the assumption that the conditional distribution of the errors is normal, the residual sum of squares for a fitted model is proportional to the log likelihood for the model (Hosmer & Lemeshow, 1989). With this in mind, it can be argued that $-2 \log(L_0)$ is analogous to the total sum of squares, and $-2 \log(L_1)$ is analogous to the residual sum of squares, in regression. This gives rise to an R^2-type measure for logistic regression (Agresti, 1990; Hosmer & Lemeshow, 1989), denoted R_L^2:

$$R_L^2 = \frac{-2 \log L_0 - (-2 \log L_1)}{-2 \log L_0}$$

For the analysis of the murder rate in 54 SMSAs (using the main effects model expressed in Equation 16), $-2 \log(L_0)$ was 74.86, while $-2 \log(L_1)$ was 54.635. Using the formula above, we arrive at an R_L^2 of .27. Although one is tempted to think of this quantity as the proportion of variance explained by the model, it is not quite correct to do so. The difficulty with this interpretation is that minus twice the log likelihood is not really an interpretable quantity. Perhaps the best that can be said is that this measure is a rough approximation for assessing predictive efficacy. Like R^2, it tends to range from 0, when the predictors are completely unrelated to the dependent variable, to 1, when a model is fitted that allows perfect prediction. The R^2 from the OLS run (using the continuous murder rate), on the other hand, was .42. R_L^2 typically underestimates the proportion of variation explained in the underlying continuous variable (Hagle & Mitchell, in press), again revealing the loss of explanatory power that results when the response is measured only at the binary level.

Measures of Ordinal Association. Another approach is to measure the association between the binary outcome of interest and the estimated conditional probabilities of event occurrence and nonoccurrence from the model. Measures of ordinal association apply whenever one variable is at least ordinal (for example, the estimated probability) and the other is nominal but has only two categories (Agresti, 1990). The closer the association between the predicted probabilities and the occurrence of the event, the higher the absolute value of the measure (the sign of the measure is usually ignored).

One such measure is gamma, which is routinely printed by the procedure LOGISTIC in SAS. For the murder rate analysis, the value of gamma is .69. This statistic has a proportional reduction in error (PRE) interpretation: In this instance it suggests that we make about 69% fewer prediction errors in predicting which of a pair of cities has a high murder rate when we use information about which city has the higher estimated probability of having a high murder rate (according to the model) than when we predict by chance alone.

A problem with gamma, however, is that it tends to overestimate the strength of relationship between estimated probabilities and status on the dependent variable. A related but better measure is Somers's D_{yx}, designed for the case in which one variable (y) is dependent upon the other (x). We can think of status on the dependent variable as "dependent" upon the estimated probability, in that we are trying to predict the first using the second. Unfortunately, Somers's D_{yx} is not printed out by logistic regression software (SAS prints a "Somers' D" but it is D_{xy}, not D_{yx}), but is not difficult to compute with programs that write out the estimated probabilities to the data file. For the SMSA analysis, Somers's D_{yx} is .35, suggesting a much more modest level of improvement in prediction than was suggested by gamma.

Cross-Validation. A final method to be considered for assessing predictive efficacy is sample cross-validation, a technique commonly used in discriminant analysis. Here, we simulate the situation in which we actually intend to "put the model to work" making predictions for new observations, on a case-by-case basis. This procedure involves randomly splitting the sample into two equal halves. One half is the prediction sample and the other is the validation sample.

The idea is to estimate the logistic regression model using the prediction sample. With this equation, we calculate the probability of event occurrence for all cases in the validation sample, based on their predictor values. If a case has a predicted probability of event occurrence that is greater than .5, it is classified as being in the category of interest. Otherwise, it is classified in the other category. We then compare predicted and actual classification on the dependent variable in the validation sample and count the number of errors made using the model to predict event occurrence. In the murder rate example, 9 out of 27 cities are incorrectly classified using this approach.

To complete the procedure, we estimate how much our predictive capability is improved using the model, over what could be obtained by chance alone. In the absence of the model, our best guess regarding status on the dependent variable would be based on the marginal distribution on the dependent variable in the prediction sample. Let p equal the marginal probability of event occurrence in the prediction sample, and p^* equal the marginal probability of event occurrence in the validation sample. The chance error rate can then be computed as $p(1 - p^*) + p^*(1 - p)$. For the murder rate analysis, 13 of the 27 cities in the prediction sample had a high murder rate (hence $p = .481$), while, for the validation sample, 14 out of 27 cities had high murder rates (hence $p^* = .519$). The probability of chance error is $.481(.481) + .519(.519) = .5$, implying that we would make $.5(27) = 13.5$ errors through chance alone. The cross-validation PRE measure is then computed as $PRE_{cv} =$ (chance errors − model errors)/chance errors = $(13.5 - 9)/13.5 = .33$. We therefore reduce our prediction errors by about a third when using the model to predict whether a city has a high murder rate. We would, of course, derive our final parameter estimates for the model from an analysis employing the full sample—in this case, all 54 SMSAs.

Some words of caution are in order. First, the method of computing chance errors advocated here assumes that prediction accuracy is desired in equal measure for each category of the dependent variable. For alternative ways of estimating the probability of chance error, I refer the reader to the discussion of discriminant analysis in Hair, Anderson, and Tatham (1987). Second, while PRE_{cv} will attain a maximum value of 1 when no errors are made using the model, it is not clear that the minimum value will be zero. It is possible, although not likely, that one can actually make fewer errors with chance prediction than when using the model. In this instance, PRE_{cv} would be negative. However, this can be remedied by simply defining PRE_{cv} to be zero whenever this occurs.

Finally, only three of several proposed measures of predictive efficacy have been discussed here. Others are outlined in Aldrich and Nelson (1984) and McKelvey and Zavoina (1975). A recent Monte Carlo simulation evaluated the performance of four "pseudo-R^2s" for use in logit and probit regression (Hagle & Mitchell, in press). The authors found that a modified version of the measure proposed by Aldrich and Nelson (1984) performed best across a range of model assumptions. However, this evaluation was based on the assumption that a dichotomous dependent variable is only a proxy for the true, interval-level dependent variable that would be available given sufficiently precise measurement. While this assumption is often a reasonable one, it would not be valid whenever the dependent variable of interest is truly binary. In sum, it may not be prudent to rely on only one measure for assessing predictive efficacy in logistic regression—particularly in view of the lack of consensus on which measure is most appropriate. Perhaps the best strategy is to report more than one measure for any given analysis. If the model has predictive power, this should be reflected in some degree by all of the measures discussed above.

Evaluating the Effects of Intervening Variables

As a final topic in this chapter, I shall consider the role of logistic regression in testing a more complex hypothesis than simply whether certain predictors are associated with a dependent variable. Structural, or path-analytic, models for interval dependent variables are frequently applied in social research (see Bollen, 1989, for a comprehensive discussion of linear structural modeling). At the core of such analyses is the hypothesis that one or more intervening variables mediate the impact of one's explanatory variables on a response. Such hypotheses are readily evaluated in linear regression by estimating models with and without the intervening variables of interest. Using an increment-to-R^2 test (Jaccard et al., 1990), the researcher then decides whether the intervening variable set adds a significant proportion to the explained variance in the dependent variable. If so, a comparison of coefficients in each equation reveals the extent to which the explanatory variables exert their effects through the intervening variables (see Alwin & Hauser, 1975, for a theoretical development and illustration of this hierarchical regression approach to the estimation of path models). The same techniques are applicable in logistic regression, except that a chi-squared difference test takes the place of the increment-to-R^2 test.

Violence in Intimate Dyads. I shall illustrate this procedure with an example drawn from my own research. The National Survey of Families and Households (NSFH) 1987-1988 (Sweet, Bumpass, & Call, 1988) contained a sequence of questions asked of both married and unmarried cohabiting couples about conflict in their relationships. The focus of my inquiry was on differences between cohabiting and married couples in the occurrence of violent confrontations between the partners. Along with others (Stets & Straus, 1989), I found that cohabitors were more likely than married couples to report that "physical arguments" had occurred in the past year.

Stets and Straus (1989) have theorized that there are three reasons cohabiting relationships are more violent. First, cohabitors are more likely than married couples to be socially isolated from their kin networks. This isolation makes it more difficult for violence to be monitored and, therefore, held in check by the kin group. Second, because cohabitation fosters greater ambiguity regarding the roles and obligations of the partners, there is more potential for conflict to erupt. Finally, married couples are characterized by greater psychological and material investment in the relationship. Consequently, compared with cohabitors, their violence is constrained more by the fear that their actions will result in the termination of the relationship.

To test whether these intervening factors account for the differences in violence between the two groups, I tested models with and without these variables. Table 4.2 shows the results of these logistic regressions for the 3,678 married and cohabiting couples in the survey with complete data on all relevant variables. The dependent variable is coded 1 if either partner to the couple reported a "physical argument" in the last year, and 2 otherwise (for PROC LOGISTIC in SAS). Independent variables are either continuous or categorical, with the latter entered as

TABLE 4.2

Logistic Regression of Couple Violence on Exogenous and Intervening Characteristics of Couples ($n = 3,678$)

Effect	Parameter Estimates Model 1	Parameter Estimates Model 2
Intercept	.554	−.049
Cohabiting	.616**	.496*
Male partner's education	−.071**	−.068**
Female partner's education	.017	−.009
Total household income	−.00015	.003
Both partners nonwhite	.482**	.328*
Partners racially mixed	.190	.078
Male's age	−.018	−.014
Female's age	−.023*	.001
No religious affiliations given	−.252	−.170
Both partners Catholic	.010	.028
Male's frequency of church attendance	−.087**	−.060*
Female's frequency of church attendance	−.001	−.005
Male's frequency of open disagreement	—	.615**
Female's frequency of open disagreement	—	.379**
Male's visitation with parents	—	.027
Male's communication with parents	—	−.042
Female's visitation with parents	—	.009
Female's communication with parents	—	.012
Duration of relationship in years	—	−.013
Male's subjective investment	—	−.127
Female's subjective investment	—	−.499**
Stepchild household	—	.117
Natural child household	—	−.251*
Economic investment	—	−.045
Model chi-squared	204.283**	406.454**
Degrees of freedom	12.0	24.0

*$p < .05$; **$p < .01$.

dummy variables. Model 1 contains the focus variable, Cohabiting, as well as several sociodemographic controls. Cohabiting is a dummy variable coded 1 for cohabitors and 0 for marrieds. The controls are male and female partners' education in years; total household income in thousands of dollars; race status of the couple, entered as two dummy variables—both partners nonwhite and partners racially mixed ("both partners white" is the reference category); male's and female's ages; religious affiliation status of the couple entered as two dummies—no religious affiliation given by male or female and both partners Catholic ("any other combination" is the reference category); and male's and female's frequencies of church attendance (each coded into 9 ordered categories, from "never" to "approximately once a week or more").

Model 2 contains all variables in Model 1 plus measures of the three intervening, or mediating, factors. The NSFH did not contain any measures of role ambiguity, as such. However, in that role ambiguity is expected to lead to greater conflict among cohabitors, I included conflict as the relevant intervening variable. The amount of conflict was measured by the male and female partners' reports of how often there had been open disagreements between the partners in the last year in the areas of household tasks, money, spending time together, sex, having a(nother) child, and in-laws. Responses ranged from 1 = "never" to 6 = "almost every day." Male's and female's "frequency of open disagreement" scores were computed as the mean responses for each partner over all six items. Frequency of contact with the kin network was measured by how often, on a 1 to 6 scale, each partner communicated with and visited his or her parents. Investment was measured in several ways. Time investment was measured by duration of the relationship, in years. Subjective investment was based upon asking each respondent how life would change for him or her in each of five areas if the relationship ended. The areas were standard of living, social life, career opportunities, overall happiness, and sex life, with responses 1 = "much better" to 5 = "much worse." Each partner's subjective investment score was the mean response over the five items. Genetic investment was assessed by determining whether there were any children in the household and, if so, whether all were the natural children of both parents. Two dummy variables were created: Stepchild Household, for couples in which at least one child was a stepchild for one of the partners, and Natural Child Household, for couples in which all children were natural children (the reference category was childless couples). Natural child households are presumed to reflect the greatest degree of genetic investment and childless households the least. Finally, Economic Investment was a dummy variable coded 1 if only one of the partners was employed—and hence was supported by the other's income—and 0 otherwise (i.e., both partners employed or both partners unemployed).

If Stets and Straus's theory is correct, I should find (a) that the intervening variables are indeed predictive of violence, and (b) that the difference between cohabitors and marrieds in the likelihood of violence is partially or wholly eliminated once the intervening variables are controlled. To establish the former, I test whether the subset of intervening variables makes a significant contribution to the model. This is equivalent to a simultaneous test of the null hypothesis that all of the coefficients of these variables are zero against the alternative that at least one is nonzero. The test is simply the difference in model chi-squareds (ΔC^2) for Model 2 versus Model 1. If the null hypothesis is true, this difference has the chi-squared distribution with df = the number of parameters set to zero in the null hypothesis. In this example, ΔC^2 is 406.54 − 204.283 = 202.171. With 12 df, the test is highly significant ($p < .0001$). It is apparent that at least one of the intervening variables has a significant impact on the log odds of violence; z tests for individual coefficients suggest that four intervening variables have significant effects. The greater the frequency of open disagreements reported by either partner, the greater the log odds of violence. The greater the female partner's subjective investment in the relationship, the lower the log odds of violence. Finally, households containing one or more children all of whom are the biological offspring of both members of the couple have lower log odds of violence than childless households.

To establish the second point, we examine the reduction in the magnitude of the parameter estimate for cohabiting between Model 1 and Model 2. In Model 1, beta is .616, while in Model 2 it is reduced to .496, a 19% reduction. Thus about a fifth of the estimated impact on violence of cohabiting, as opposed to being married, is accounted for by conflict, isolation, and investment. Stets and Straus's theory is therefore supported to some degree, although it does not completely account for cohabitors' higher likelihood of violence.

The estimate of predictive efficacy for the complete model (Model 2) varies considerably across the three measures discussed above. The coefficients for R_L^2, Dyx, and PRE_{cv} are, respectively, .14, .12, and .46. Apparently, "putting the model to work" results in a substantially higher estimate of its predictive usefulness than is obtained from either R_L^2 or Dyx.

5. ADVANCED TOPICS
IN LOGISTIC REGRESSION

The previous chapters have all been concerned with binary response variables. In this chapter, logit techniques are applied to the case of a polytomous dependent variable. First to be considered is the situation in which the values of the dependent variable are either inherently unordered or more properly treated as being unordered. Subsequently, the focus will be the case in which the dependent variable is truly ordinal, and an appropriate model will be presented that is based upon the construction of cumulative logits. The chapter concludes with some general remarks about logit modeling.

Polytomous Logistic Regression

Logit modeling is not limited to binary dependent variables. Whenever the dependent variable is qualitative and has three or more categories, logits can be formed from contrasts of nonredundant category pairs. Each logit is then modeled in a separate equation. The technique is referred to as *polytomous* or *multinomial logistic regression*. Traditionally, polytomous dependent variables have been handled with discriminant analysis. Polytomous logistic regression may be preferable, however, because it is a natural extension of logistic regression for a binary response, its results are more interpretable, and there is no requirement that the predictor set have the multivariate normal distribution (Press & Wilson, 1978).

I shall develop the technique with an example. The NSFH contained a question concerning the perceived fairness of household task allocation. This was asked of all respondents living with an intimate partner, regardless of marital status. The question was "How do you feel about the fairness in your relationship in each of the following areas?" This was followed by a list of several areas, one of which was "household chores." The response categories were "very unfair to me," "somewhat unfair to me," "fair to both," "somewhat unfair to partner," and "very unfair to partner." This variable will be referred to as the Perceived Fairness of Task Allocation. I am interesting in modeling a woman's response to this item, as a function of several predictors.

How to proceed from here depends upon whether the levels of this variable are perceived to be ordered or unordered. This issue is not as straightforward as might be assumed at first glance. One might, for example, consider this variable to be ordinal, with responses that range from very unadvantageous to the female partner ("very unfair to me") to very advantageous to the female partner ("very unfair to the partner"). That being the case, the appropriate analysis would be ordered logit regression, as explained below. However, in view of developments in equity theory, this would not be a theoretically sophisticated strategy.

To begin with, the construct of interest, *fairness,* reaches its zenith when both partners are equally "advantaged," not when the advantage is all in favor of one partner. Consequently, the highest level of fairness is represented by the response "fair to both." This perception is shared by equity theorists, who distinguish qualitatively between two types of inequity, depending upon which partner has the advantage in the relationship. Hence the woman who responds "very unfair to me" or "somewhat unfair to me" is *underbenefited,* while the woman who responds "somewhat unfair to partner" or "very unfair to partner" is *overbenefited.* It is therefore desirable to examine not only whether inequity exists in relationships, but also what type of inequity is present. Moreover, the fact that different types of inequity manifest different effects on other outcomes underscores the importance of this qualitative distinction (Sprecher, 1986). With this in mind, the analysis of this variable will be accomplished by collapsing the first two responses into Category 1, "Unfair to Respondent" (female partner underbenefited), while the last two responses will be collapsed into Category 2, "Unfair to Partner" (female partner overbenefited). "Fair to Both" is Category 3. This results in a three-category qualitative (i.e., unordered) dependent variable representing the type of inequity in the relationship with respect to task allocation.

Panel A of Table 5.1 shows the cross-tabulation of fairness of household chores with respondent's race for the 2,824 married or cohabiting women in the NSFH with complete data on several predictors of interest. I shall for the moment consider only one predictor, to demonstrate how odds ratios are formed in the polytomous situation. Subsequently, I shall extend the example to the case in which there are several predictors, one or more of which are continuous.

There are two independent odds that can be formed from contrasts of fairness response categories. One is the odds that a woman perceives task allocation as unfair to herself instead of fair to both, denoted O_1^F. Based on the marginal row totals, this is estimated to be $853/1857 = .459$ for the sample as a whole. A second is the odds that a woman perceives task allocation as unfair to her partner instead of fair to both, denoted O_2^F and estimated as $114/1857 = .061$. The third possible contrast—the odds that task allocation is perceived as unfair to the respondent instead of unfair to the partner, is simply the ratio of the first two odds, and is therefore not independent: $853/114 = [(853/1857)/(114/1857)] = 7.482$. In general, if there are M categories of the dependent variable, only $M - 1$ independent odds can be formed, although a total of $M(M - 1)/2$ possible odds can be examined.

TABLE 5.1

Cross-Tabulation of Fairness of Household Chores With Respondent's Race for 2,824 Married and Cohabiting Women, and Odds Ratios for All Race Contrasts on Fairness

A. Cross-Tabulation

Fairness	Black	Race Hispanic	White	Total
Unfair to Respondent	95	48	710	853
%	32.4	21.2	30.8	
Unfair to Partner	16	16	82	114
%	5.5	7.1	3.6	
Fair to Both	182	163	1512	1857
%	62.1	71.7	65.6	
Total	293	227	2304	2824

B. Odds Ratios

Fairness Contrasts	Black vs. White	Race Contrasts Hispanic vs. White	Black vs. Hispanic
Unfair to Respondent vs. Fair to Both	1.112	.627**	1.773**
Unfair to Partner vs. Fair to Both	1.621	1.809*	.896
Unfair to Respondent vs. Unfair to Partner	.686	.346**	1.979

*Significantly different from 1 at $p < .05$; **significantly different from 1 at $p < .01$.

Overall, the association between race and fairness is significant ($X^2 = 16.67, p = .002$). Each of the three possible odds can be used to form odds ratios, based on contrasts between categories of race. These contrasts can further illuminate the ways in which racial groups differ in the perception of fairness of household tasks. For example, the odds ratio for blacks (Category 1 of race) versus whites (Category 3), based on O_1^F, is

$$\frac{O_{11}^{FR}}{O_{13}^{FR}} = \frac{95/182}{710/1512} = 1.112.$$

This is the ratio of the odds of perceiving chores as unfair to the respondent (as opposed to fair to both) for blacks versus whites. Because it is barely greater than one, it appears that the odds of perceiving chores as unfair to the respondent are about the same for blacks and whites. Moreover, this ratio is not significantly different from 1 (how to do this test will be described shortly), further supporting this judgment.

In contrast, the odds ratio for Hispanics (Category 2) versus whites is

$$\frac{O_{12}^{FR}}{O_{13}^{FR}} = \frac{48/163}{710/1512} = 0.627.$$

The odds of perceiving chores as unfair to the respondent are thus only about 63% as high for Hispanics as for whites. Moreover, this difference is significant at $p < .01$. The odds ratio for blacks versus Hispanics is 1.773, the ratio of the first two odds. This ratio is also significantly different from 1 at $p < .01$. Similar odds ratios can be computed for the other odds of interest—the odds of perceiving chores as unfair to the partner (as opposed to fair to both), and the odds of perceiving chores as unfair to the respondent as opposed to unfair to the partner. The nine odds ratios and their significance levels are indicated in panel B of Table 5.1 (note that once the first four odds ratios in the first two rows and the first two columns are computed, all other odds ratios can be derived from these by division). Substantively, it appears that Hispanic women have lower odds of seeing household tasks as unfair to them than do either white or black women, and higher odds of seeing them as unfair to the partner than do white women.

One caution should be mentioned regarding polytomous logits. An examination of the conditional percentages in panel A of Table 5.1 reveals that black women are more likely than their white counterparts to see chores as unfair, regardless of the direction of unfairness. Thus 32.4% of black women, compared with 30.8% of white women, see chores as unfair to the respondent, and 5.5% of black women versus 3.6% of white women view chores as unfair to the partner. The odds ratios in panel B for the independent odds reflect this relationship: The odds that blacks see tasks as unfair to the respondent or unfair to the partner (as opposed to fair to both) are, respectively, 1.112 and 1.621 times the same odds for whites. However, the third odds ratio, contrasting the odds of seeing tasks as unfair to the respondent with the odds of seeing them as unfair to the partner, for blacks versus whites, suggests that blacks have *lower* odds of seeing chores as unfair to the respondent. While this appears to be a contradiction, it only reflects the conditional nature of polytomous logits (Theil, 1970). That is, the logits are conditional on being in one of the two categories from which they are constructed. In the example, blacks are more likely to be in either category of unfairness, compared with whites. But, *among all those who perceive chores as unfair*, the odds of perceiving them as unfair to the respondent (as opposed to unfair to the partner) are lower for blacks than for whites. Because this has the potential to be quite confusing, I recommend limiting an analysis to an examination of only the independent odds. As the choice of category for the denominator of these odds is arbitrary, it becomes incumbent upon the analyst to choose a category that facilitates interpretation. Here, I have chosen to use "Fair to Both" as the reference category for the independent odds, partly because it is the modal response, and partly because I wish to examine what predictors are associated with perceptions of unfairness.

The Model. The independent odds can be elegantly described in terms of the polytomous logistic regression model. We construct a separate logistic regression equation for the log of each odds, and estimate the parameters via maximum likelihood. Race is included as two dummy variables, with "white" as the contrast (omitted) group. The equations are as follows:

$$\log O_1^F = \alpha^1 + \delta_1^1 (\text{BLACK}) + \delta_2^1 (\text{HISPANIC}),$$

$$\log O_2^F = \alpha^2 + \delta_1^2 (\text{BLACK}) + \delta_2^2 (\text{HISPANIC}).$$

The superscripts on the parameters serve to distinguish effects that relate to the first odds from those that relate to the second. We could write an equation for the third, dependent, odds—the odds of perceiving chores as unfair to the respondent as opposed to unfair to the partner. However, there is no need to estimate the third equation from the data, because its parameters are just the differences between parameters in the first two equations.

Polytomous logistic regression can be accomplished with the procedure CATMOD in SAS. The program for estimating these two equations is given in Table A.5 in the Appendix (where CHORES is the variable name for "fairness of task allocation"). The results (not shown) provide the following estimates for the equations above:

$$\log O_1^F = -0.756 + 0.106 (\text{BLACK}) - 0.467 (\text{HISPANIC}),$$

$$\log O_2^F = -2.914 + 0.483 (\text{BLACK}) + 0.593 (\text{HISPANIC}).$$

The odds ratios in panel B of Table 5.1 are readily recovered from these equations by exponentiating the dummy coefficients, or deltas. For example, $\exp(\hat{\delta}_1^1) = \exp(.106) = 1.112$ is the ratio of the odds of perceiving chores as unfair to the respondent for blacks versus whites. The ratio for Hispanics versus whites is $\exp(-.467) = .627$. The odds ratio for blacks versus Hispanics is obtained by exponentiating the difference between the deltas: $\exp[.106 - (-.467)] = 1.773$. Similar operations recover the other odds ratios in the table.

SAS provides significance tests for each dummy coefficient, thereby revealing the significance of the odds ratios for blacks versus whites and for Hispanics versus whites. A test for the significance of the odds ratio for blacks versus Hispanics is a z test for the significance of the difference between deltas. The variance of this difference (for the first odds) is, by covariance algebra,

$$V(\hat{\delta}_1^1 - \hat{\delta}_2^1) = V(\hat{\delta}_1^1) + V(\hat{\delta}_2^1) - 2\text{Cov}(\hat{\delta}_1^1, \hat{\delta}_2^1) \, .$$

Similar algebra is needed to provide standard errors for the odds ratios contrasting blacks and Hispanics with whites on the third, dependent, odds. The contrast between blacks and Hispanics on the third odds requires some tedious algebra, because one must find the estimated variance of a linear combination of four parameter estimates. Estimates of the variances and covariances for these computations are obtained from the covariance matrix of parameter estimates.

Multiple Predictors. The foregoing discussion has been based upon the inclusion of only one predictor, for simplicity. In practice, we would realistically want to include several predictors, with some of them possibly measured at the interval level. In general, the multiple polytomous logistic regression model for a categorical dependent variable with M levels is a series of $M - 1$ equations, one for each independent odds, with each equation consisting of an intercept and K predictors. Assuming that the last, or Mth, category of the dependent variable is the reference category, the equations are of the form:

$$\log O_1 = \alpha^1 + \beta_1^1 X_1 + \beta_2^1 X_2 + \ldots + \beta_K^1 X_K \, ,$$

$$\log O_2 = \alpha^2 + \beta_1^2 X_1 + \beta_2^2 X_2 + \ldots + \beta_K^2 X_K \, ,$$

$$\vdots$$

$$\log O_{M-1} = \alpha^{M-1} + \beta_1^{M-1} X_1 + \beta_2^{M-1} X_2 + \ldots + \beta_K^{M-1} X_K \, .$$

The Xs in the equations above can be either continuous or dummy variables.

As in logistic regression with a binary response, parameters are estimated by maximizing the likelihood function for the sample responses on the dependent variable. This function expresses the conditional distribution on the dependent variable, given the predictor set, in terms of the parameters in the $M - 1$ equations. Also, as in the binary case, there is a global test for the significance of the predictor set. The null hypothesis is that all $K(M - 1)$ betas included in the $M - 1$ logit equations are simultaneously equal to zero. The alternative hypothesis is that at least one of these betas is nonzero. The test is a model chi-squared statistic, C^2, equal to $-2\log(L_0) - [-2\log(L_1)]$, where L_0 is the likelihood function evaluated at the MLEs of the parameters under the null hypothesis (in which the only parameters are the intercepts), and L_1 is the likelihood function evaluated at the MLEs of the parameters under the alternative hypothesis (in which the parameter set includes all of the betas as well). This is a chi-squared test with $K(M - 1)$ degrees of freedom. If the test is significant, we reject H_0 and conclude that at least one predictor has a significant impact on at least one of the logits.

There are two possible tests for the "effect" of a given predictor: (a) a global test for the impact of the predictor on the dependent variable, in general, and (b) a test for the impact of the predictor on a given logit. The null hypothesis for the first, or global, test is that all $M - 1$ betas associated with a particular predictor are simultaneously zero. For example, in the equations above, the global test for the variable X_1 tests the null hypothesis that

$$\beta_1^1 = \beta_1^2 = \ldots = \beta_1^{M-1} = 0 .$$

That is, X_1 has no effect on any of the $M - 1$ logits. The test is a ΔC^2 test based on the difference in C^2 between the full model, with all predictors, and the reduced model, with all predictors except X_1. The test has $M - 1$ degrees of freedom; if it is significant, then X_1 has a significant impact on the dependent variable. This test, for each of the predictors in the model, is a standard part of CATMOD output.

The second test is used to determine which logits are significantly affected by X_1. Assuming that the sample size is sufficiently large, each coefficient estimate divided by its standard error is a z test for the impact of a given predictor in a particular equation. Thus a test for whether X_1

has a significant impact on the odds of being in the first, as opposed to the last, category of the independent variable is

$$z = \frac{\hat{\beta}_1^1}{\text{SE}(\hat{\beta}_1^1)}.$$

Similar tests apply to each of the coefficients for X_1 in the other equations. If the global test for X_1 is significant, one or more, but perhaps not all, of these tests will also be significant. Thus X_1 may be found to be globally significant but its effect may be important in only one of the logit equations. These tests are also provided by SAS.

A third type of test, which is not automatically provided by SAS, is a test for a subset of predictors. For example, suppose that X_1 and X_2 in the equations above are dummy variables representing a categorical predictor. CATMOD would automatically provide a test for the global impact of each *dummy variable* separately on the dependent variable; each test would be a chi-squared test with $M - 1$ degrees of freedom. But a global test for the impact of the *categorical predictor* on the dependent variable is a ΔC^2 test based on the difference in C^2 for the full model, containing both dummies, and the reduced model, without the dummies. This test has $2(M - 1)$ degrees of freedom. This can be performed by separately estimating the full and reduced models, and then taking $\Delta C^2 = -2\log(L_2) - [-2\log(L_1)]$, where L_2 is the likelihood function evaluated at the MLEs of the parameters in the reduced model. SAS always provides minus twice the log of the likelihood function for the current model, so this test is readily calculated from CATMOD output.

An Example. Returning to the fairness of household chores, Table 5.2 shows the results of estimating models for the log odds of perceiving chores as unfair to the respondent, and for the log odds of perceiving chores as unfair to the partner ("Fair to Both" is the reference category, as before), as a function of several explanatory variables. Race is once again included, along with whether the respondent is currently cohabiting outside of marriage ("Respondent Is Married" is the contrast category), total household income (in thousands), whether the respondent is employed ("Unemployed" is the contrast category), respondent's completed years of education, the number of children in the household, and the duration of the relationship in years.

TABLE 5.2

Polytomous Logistic Regression of Fairness of Household Chores on Predictor Set for 2,824 Married and Cohabiting Women

A. *Global Tests for Effects of Predictors*

Effect	df	ΔC^2	p
Intercept	2	53.91	.0001
Respondent is cohabiting	2	.40	.8199
Respondent is black	2	2.61	.2714
Respondent is Hispanic	2	14.15	.0008
Total household income	2	4.34	.1139
Respondent is employed	2	35.27	.0001
Respondent's education	2	.61	.7370
Number of children in household	2	24.69	.0001
Duration of relationship	2	17.29	.0002

B. *Individual Effects on Log Odds*

Effect	Odds That Chores Are Unfair to Respondent	Odds That Chores Are Unfair to Partner
Intercept	−1.411**	−3.103**
Respondent is cohabiting	.024	.219
Respondent is black	.014	.465
Respondent is Hispanic	−.487**	.688*
Total household income	.005*	.003
Respondent is employed	.540**	.322
Respondent's education	.014	.016
Number of children in household	.164**	−.045
Duration of relationship	−.014**	−.020*

*p < .05; **p < .01.

The global chi-squared test for the significance of the predictor set is 148.23 with 16 df, which is highly significant.[8] Panel A of the table shows the global tests (ΔC^2s) for the effects of each predictor on the dependent variable. Respondent's employment, number of children in the household, and duration of the relationship all have significant effects. The test for the global impact of race, based on estimating models with and without the two race dummies (results not shown) is $\Delta C^2 = 15.54$ (df = 4, p = .0037). As this is highly significant, it can be concluded that race has a significant impact on the perceived fairness of household chores. From the tests in panel A, however, it is apparent that the contrasts between Hispanics and whites are primarily responsible for producing this result.

One reason for adding several other demographic variables here might be to examine whether observed race differences reflected in the odds ratios in Table 5.1 can be explained by these factors. We might be particularly interested in explaining why Hispanic women tend to see household tasks as more equitably distributed or more unfair to the partner, compared with black or white women. One possibility is that Hispanic women are more traditional than others with respect to marital roles. Hence they may have less formal education and be less likely to be employed outside the home. These factors, in turn, would be expected to be positively associated with the odds of perceiving the status quo—in which it is assumed that women will shoulder most of the burden of household tasks—as unfair. If this reasoning is correct, the odds ratios that compare Hispanics with other women, in panel B of Table 5.1, should become closer to 1—showing a weaker impact for being Hispanic—when these factors are controlled.

This does not turn out to be the case, however. Panel B of Table 5.2 presents the logit coefficients for each independent odds. Of the three contrasts involving the independent odds, which were found to be significant in Table 5.1, one odds ratio is now slightly closer to 1, but the other two are further from 1. The adjusted ratio of the odds of perceiving chores as unfair to the respondent for blacks versus Hispanics is now $\exp[.014 - (-.487)] = 1.65$ instead of 1.773, but is still significant at $p < .05$ (after applying covariance algebra to obtain the standard error of the difference between coefficients). On the other hand, the adjusted odds ratios for Hispanics versus whites are now $\exp(-.487) = .614$ and $\exp(.688) = 1.99$ for the first and second odds, respectively, as opposed to .627 and 1.809 without controls for other factors. It appears, therefore, that the aforementioned differences between Hispanics and other women are not explained by variables in the model.

Of the other significant effects on the odds, most pertain to the odds of perceiving chores as unfair to the respondent. Respondents who are employed have estimated odds of perceiving chores as unfair to the respondent that are $\exp(.540) = 1.716$ times the odds for those who are not employed. Each additional $1,000 in household income is estimated to increase the odds of perceiving chores as unfair to the respondent by a factor of $\exp(.005) = 1.005$. In that the global test for household income was not quite significant, the conservative approach would be to ignore the test for this coefficient. Each additional child is estimated to increase the odds of perceiving chores as unfair to the respondent by a factor of 1.178. Duration of the relationship seems to affect the odds of perceiving either type of unfairness: the longer couples are together, the lower the odds that the female partner perceives chores as being unfair to either partner.

Estimating Conditional Probabilities. Estimated probabilities, conditioned on a given combination of predictor values, for each category of the dependent variable are easily recovered from the logit equations. In the current example, if U_1 is the estimated log odds of perceiving chores as unfair to the respondent, and U_2 is the estimated log odds of perceiving chores as unfair to the partner, for a given covariate pattern, then the estimated conditional probabilities are given by

$$P(\text{unfair to respondent}) = \frac{e^{U_1}}{1 + e^{U_1} + e^{U_2}},$$

$$P(\text{unfair to partner}) = \frac{e^{U_2}}{1 + e^{U_1} + e^{U_2}},$$

$$P(\text{fair to both}) = \frac{1}{1 + e^{U_1} + e^{U_2}}.$$

Ordered Logit Modeling

When the dependent variable is both polytomous and ordinal, it makes sense to form logits that take advantage of the ordered nature of the categories. While there is more than one way to do this, I shall focus on the use of *cumulative logits* (for alternative formulations, see Agresti, 1989, 1990; McKelvey & Zavoina, 1975). These are particularly appropriate when the construct underlying the ordinal measure is actually continuous, at least in the theoretical domain (Agresti, 1989). Cumulative logits are defined as follows. Suppose that the dependent variable consists of J ordered categories, represented by the integers $1, 2, \ldots, J$. The jth cumulative odds is the probability of giving a response in category j or lower, as opposed to giving a response in category $j + 1$ or higher. That is, if we let $O_{\leq j}$ be the jth cumulative odds, and π_j be the probability of giving a response in category j, then we have that

$$O_{\leq j} = \frac{\pi_1 + \pi_2 + \ldots + \pi_j}{\pi_{j+1} + \ldots + \pi_J}.$$

72

TABLE 5.3
Cross-Tabulation of Type of Premarital Cohabitation With Marital Instability for 2,023 Couples in Their First Marriages

A. *Cross-Tabulation*

| | Marital Instability | | |
Type of Premarital Cohabitation	Very Unstable	Somewhat Unstable	Stable
Single-instance cohabitation	107	48	204
Serial cohabitation	50	25	67
No cohabitation	327	218	977
Total	484	291	1248

B. *Odds Ratios*

| | Premarital Cohabitation Contrasts | | |
Cumulative Odds	Single-Instance vs. None	Serial vs. None	Single-Instance vs. Serial
Very unstable vs. other	1.552**	1.986**	.781
Very or somewhat unstable vs. stable	1.362**	2.007**	.679

**Significantly different from 1 at $p < .01$.

The log of this odds is the jth cumulative logit. There are a total of $J - 1$ such logits that can be formed from a J-category variable. Moreover, the logits are ordered, because the probabilities in the numerators of the odds keep accumulating as we go from construction of the first through construction of the $(J - 1)$th logit. Thus, if U_j is the jth cumulative logit, the ordered property is such that $U_1 \leq U_2 \leq \ldots \leq U_{J-1}$.

An Example. Panel A of Table 5.3 presents the cross-tabulation of type of premarital cohabitation with marital instability for 2,023 couples in the NSFH who were in their first marriages and who had been married for up to 20 years' duration. The dependent variable, Marital Instability, refers to the inclination of the couple toward eventual termination of the marriage. It is ordinal, with levels 1 = very unstable, 2 = somewhat unstable, and 3 = stable. Premarital cohabitation was characterized as being one of three types: no premarital cohabitation, single-instance cohabitation (both partners had cohabited only with each other before marrying), or serial cohabitation (at least one of the partners had cohabited with someone besides the spouse before marrying). Prior research led to the expectation that both types of cohabitation would be associated with greater instability. Cohabitation appears to be selective of nontraditional individuals, who are also more prone to have unstable marriages. Moreover, because serial cohabitation is especially selective of these types of people, its association with instability should be even more pronounced than is the case for single-instance cohabitation.

To begin, we form the two cumulative odds: $O_{\leq 1}$, the odds of being very unstable as opposed to being either somewhat unstable or stable; and $O_{\leq 2}$, the odds of being either very or somewhat unstable as opposed to being stable. The highest category whose probability is accumulated in the numerator is referred to as the "cutpoint" category. Hence the cutpoint categories for the two odds are, respectively, 1 (very unstable) and 2 (somewhat unstable). Marginally, these odds are, respectively, $484/(291 + 1248) = .314$, and $(484 + 291)/1248 = .621$. To examine the relationship between type of cohabitation and marital instability, we form odds ratios for contrasts between categories of cohabitation, based on each of these odds. For example, the ratio of the odds of being very unstable, as opposed to being either somewhat unstable or stable, for single-instance cohabitors versus noncohabitors is

$$\frac{107/(48 + 204)}{327/(218 + 977)} = 1.552.$$

On the other hand, the ratio of the odds of being very or somewhat unstable, as opposed to being stable, for single-instance cohabitors versus noncohabitors is

$$\frac{(107 + 48)/204}{(327 + 218)/977} = 1.362.$$

Similar operations result in the other four odds ratios depicted in panel B of Table 5.3.

Each of the two odds formed from categories of the dependent variable is the odds of having a more, rather than a less, unstable marriage. Based upon an examination of the odds ratios in panel B, it can be said in summary that cohabitors, regardless of type of cohabitation, tend to have higher odds of having a more unstable marriage than do noncohabitors. However, as expected, serial cohabitors have higher odds of having more unstable marriages than do single-instance cohabitors.

The Model. The ordered logit model is simply a set of equations for each cumulative logit. In the example, the two equations are as follows:

$$\log O_{\leq 1} = \alpha^1 + \delta_1^1 \text{(Single-Instance)} + \delta_2^1 \text{(Serial)},$$

$$\log O_{\leq 2} = \alpha^2 + \delta_1^2 \text{(Single-Instance)} + \delta_2^2 \text{(Serial)}.$$

As in the polytomous logit model, the superscripts serve to distinguish the parameters pertaining to different cumulative logits. Estimation is quite straightforward using any program that performs logistic regression on binary dependent variables. One simply constructs dichotomous variables representing each bifurcation of the ordinal variable, based upon a different cutpoint category. In this example, I let the variable VUNST equal 1 if the couple is very unstable and 2 otherwise, and I let the variable SMWUNST equal 1 if the couple is either very unstable or somewhat unstable and 2 otherwise. Each resulting binary dependent variable is then regressed on the dummy variables representing cohabitation type. The estimated equations are as follows (estimated asymptotic standard errors in parentheses):

$$\log \hat{O}_{\leq 1} = -1.2959 + 0.4393 \text{(Single-Instance)} + 0.6862 \text{(Serial)},$$
$$\phantom{\log \hat{O}_{\leq 1} = -1.2959 + } (0.1312) \phantom{\text{(Single-Instance)} + } (0.1865)$$

$$\log \hat{O}_{\leq 2} = -0.5837 + 0.3090 \text{(Single-Instance)} + 0.6965 \text{(Serial)}.$$
$$\phantom{\log \hat{O}_{\leq 2} = -0.5837 + } (0.1192) \phantom{\text{(Single-Instance)} + } (0.1764)$$

The odds ratios for cohabitors versus noncohabitors in panel B of Table 5.3 are obtained by exponentiating the estimated dummy coefficients in these equations. For example, the first odds ratio in the table is exp(.4393) = 1.552, the second is exp(.6862) = 1.986, and so forth. The significance of an odds ratio is given by the significance test for the estimated dummy coefficient; all odds ratios for cohabitors versus noncohabitors are significant at $p < .01$. The odds ratios for single-instance versus serial cohabitors are obtained by exponentiating differences between dummy coefficients. Thus, for the first odds, this ratio is exp(.4393 − .6862) = .781. A test of the significance of this ratio is achieved by testing the difference between the coefficient estimates. This requires the use of covariance algebra with the estimated variances and covariances of the parameter estimates. After doing these computations, it turns out that the contrast between single-instance and serial cohabitors is not significant for either cumulative odds.

Invariance to the Cutpoint. It should be evident that the estimated effects for each type of cohabitation are quite similar across equations.

The coefficients for the effect of single-instance cohabitation are .4393 and .3090 for the first and second cumulative logit, respectively, while the effects for serial cohabitation are even closer in value: .6862 and .6965, respectively. In fact, more often than not, this will be the case. That is, the effects of the predictors will tend to be invariant to the choice of cutpoint category. Provided that this situation holds, the model can be made much more parsimonious by incorporating this invariance into the equation:

$$\log O_{\leq j} = \alpha^j + \delta_1 (\text{Single-Instance}) + \delta_2 (\text{Serial}), \qquad \text{for } j = 1, 2.$$

Now there are two intercepts, one for each cutpoint, but only one set of parameters representing the effects of the predictors. Each delta represents the effect on the cumulative logits of being in a particular category of cohabitation. That these are invariant to cutpoint category implies that the effect of each category of cohabitation on the log odds of being more, rather than less, unstable is the same, regardless of how "more" and "less" unstable are defined.

This type of model is readily estimated using SAS. (See Table A.6 in the Appendix for the computer routine, in which UNSTAB is marital instability, SPOUSE is a dummy for single-instance cohabitation, and SPLUS is a dummy for serial cohabitation.) The estimated equation is as follows (estimated asymptotic standard errors in parentheses):

$$\log \hat{O}_{\leq j} = \{-1.2773, -0.5900\} + 0.3512 (\text{Single-Instance}) + 0.6877 (\text{Serial}).$$
$$(0.1150) \qquad\qquad\qquad (0.1669)$$

The intercepts in braces are, respectively, the intercepts for the first and second cutpoints. The parameter estimates are interpreted as follows. The intercepts are the estimated log odds of scoring less than or equal to each of the two cutpoint categories, 1 (very unstable) and 2 (somewhat unstable), for noncohabitors. Therefore, $\exp(-1.2773) = .279$ is the estimated odds of having a very unstable (as opposed to more stable) marriage, and $\exp(-.5900) = .554$ is the estimated odds of having a very unstable or somewhat unstable (as opposed to stable) marriage, for noncohabitors. The ratio of the odds of having a more unstable (as opposed to more stable) marriage for single-instance cohabitors versus noncohabitors is estimated to be $\exp(.3512) = 1.421$, while the estimated odds ratio for serial cohabitors versus noncohabitors is $\exp(.6877) = 1.989$. Because both of the dummy coefficients are significant (at $p < .01$), both of these odds ratios are significantly different from 1. The estimated odds ratio for single-instance, versus serial, cohabitors is exp(.3512 − .6877) = .714, which is not significantly different from 1 (after applying covariance algebra to obtain the standard error of the difference between these estimates). These odds ratios are constant across the two cutpoints used to distinguish "more unstable" from "more stable" marriages.

SAS provides a test for the null hypothesis that the effects are independent of cutpoint category. The test is called the Score Test for the Proportional Odds Assumption on the printout, and is a chi-squared test with degrees of freedom equal to $K(J − 2)$, where K is the number of predictors in the model. The degrees of freedom are equal to the difference in the numbers of parameters required to specify models with, as opposed to without, the invariance assumption. If the test is nonsignificant, the invariance assumption is plausible. In the current example, the chi-squared value is 2.1307, (df = 2, p = .3446), suggesting that the effects are, indeed, independent of cutpoint category.

The Multivariate Model. For K predictors, the general model that assumes effect invariance over cutpoint categories is

$$\log O_{\leq j} = \alpha^j + \beta_1 X_1 + \beta_2 X_2 + \ldots + \beta_K X_K, \qquad \text{for } j = 1, 2, \ldots, J - 1 .$$

For each predictor in the equation, $\exp(\beta_k)$ is the estimated ratio of the odds of scoring lower, rather than higher, on the dependent variable for those who are a unit apart on the predictor, controlling for other variables in the model. Returning to the current example, I have reestimated the model after adding three more explanatory variables: duration of the marriage in years, wife's age at marriage, and number of children in the household. It was of interest to see if the differences in marital instability between cohabitors and noncohabitors might be accounted for by differences on these other demographic factors (we will see that this is not the case). Due to missing values on the other predictors, the sample size was reduced, slightly, to 2,010.

The test for the proportional odds assumption was nonsignificant (chi-squared = 7.5751, df = 5, p = .1813), suggesting that the assumption of invariant effects is reasonable. Moreover, the global chi-squared test for the predictor set was 44.404 with 5 df, which is highly significant. The estimated logit equation is as follows (estimated asymptotic standard errors in parentheses):

$$\log \hat{O}_{\leq j} = \{-0.0283, 0.6686\} + 0.3651\,(\text{Single-Instance}) + 0.8009\,(\text{Serial})$$
$$\phantom{\log \hat{O}_{\leq j} = \{-0.0283, 0.6686\} + }(0.1210)\phantom{(\text{Single-Instance}) + }(0.1773)$$

$$-0.0155\,(\text{Duration}) - 0.0553\,(\text{Wife's Age at Marriage}) + 0.0523\,(\text{Children})\,.$$
$$(0.0096)\phantom{(\text{Duration}) - }(0.0126)\phantom{(\text{Wife's Age at Marriage}) + }(0.0411)$$

The coefficients for both types of cohabitation are again highly significant, as is the coefficient for wife's age at marriage (all at $p < .01$). Neither of the other predictors is significant. The odds of having a more unstable, as opposed to a more stable, marriage are estimated to be reduced by a factor of $\exp(-.0553) = .946$, or about 5%, for each additional year the bride waits before marrying. Controlling for the other predictors, the ratio of the odds of having a more unstable marriage for single-instance cohabitors versus noncohabitors is about the same as in the bivariate case—1.441, compared with 1.421. However, the difference between serial cohabitors and noncohabitors has grown: The odds ratio is now 2.228, compared with 1.989 in the bivariate case. Correspondingly, the contrast between single-instance and serial cohabitors has also grown: The odds ratio is now .648, compared with .714. This odds ratio is now significant at $p < .05$ (again, covariance algebra is required for this test). While the discussion of both polytomous and ordered logit models here has been limited to main-effects models, interaction terms are readily incorporated into both types of analyses (for further examples, see DeMaris, 1991).

Summary of Model Assumptions. Once again, let me summarize the assumptions required for using the techniques outlined in this and the previous chapter, pertaining to disaggregated data. Logistic regression assumes, first, that the dependent variable is categorical, with either unordered or ordered categories. As the number of ordered levels increases, however (beyond, say, four levels), it may be safe to use OLS regression instead of ordered logit regression. If the researcher is in doubt, he or she could use both techniques. If no substantive differences emerge from the analyses, OLS would be an acceptable approach. If differences emerge, the ordered logit approach should probably be followed. Second, it is assumed that the observations are independent of each other. Third, it is assumed that the conditional probabilities of event occurrence, which are the bases of the logits used in the model, are related to the explanatory variables through the logistic distribution function. Alternative functions are available (Aldrich & Nelson, 1984; Hanushek & Jackson, 1977); however, in practice, they are not likely to make much difference in one's substantive conclusions. Fourth, it is assumed that the predictors are fixed by design, or that they can safely be treated as though they were fixed by design. Fifth, the sample size is assumed to be "large," so that the asymptotic properties of maximum likelihood estimators are applicable. In the absence of firm guidelines, I recommend the same rule of thumb as that used for OLS regression: One should have approximately 15 cases per predictor for a reliable analysis (Stevens, 1986). Finally, it is assumed that no exact linear dependencies exist among the explanatory variables.

Concluding Comments

This monograph is intended to provide the reader with a thorough and statistically correct, albeit nonrigorous, introduction to logit modeling. With this in mind, I have presented and illustrated a variety of models that can be used for the analysis of a categorical dependent variable. Logit models for contingency-table data are appropriate for binary dependent variables in combination with nominal or ordinal independent variables. Logistic regression is useful when one or more of one's predictors are continuous. Polytomous dependent variables are best handled using either polytomous logistic regression or ordered logit regression, regardless of the level of measurement of one's explanatory variables.

The emphasis throughout this work has been on application and interpretation, primarily because these aspects of logit modeling are de-emphasized in the more technical literature. Nevertheless, the reader should understand that, because of limited space, some topics have had to be given only superficial coverage here, and others have been omitted entirely. The reader who intends to become a knowledgeable user is advised to continue his or her education in logit modeling by perusing one or more of the sources listed in the references. The reader is also encouraged to keep abreast of new developments in this field via such journals as *Psychological Bulletin, Sociological Methods & Research,* the *American Journal of Political Science*, or similar journals in his or her discipline.

APPENDIX:
COMPUTER ROUTINES FOR CHAPTERS 2-5

The following tables present the SPSS (Release 4.0), BMDP (1988 Version), and SAS (Version 6.0) programs that were used to derive the results shown in Chapters 2 through 5. These programs are intended to be examples that, when used in combination with the relevant software manuals, should facilitate the learning of logit programming. Naturally, the user will need to consult these manuals to make complete sense of the programs listed below. The SPSS program in Table A.1 and the BMDP program in Table A.2 demonstrate how to enter contingency tables directly into a program as data.

TABLE A.1
SPSS Program and Partial Output for Table 2.6

```
DATA LIST LIST/ POLVIEWS CHOICE SEX FREQ
VALUE LABELS POLVIEWS 1 'LIBERAL' 2 'MODERATE' 3 'CONSERV'/
                CHOICE 1 'BUSH' 2 'DUKA'/
                SEX 1 'MALE' 2 'FEMALE'/
WEIGHT BY FREQ
LOGLINEAR CHOICE (1,2) BY POLVIEWS (1,3) SEX (1,2)/
     PRINT = ESTIM COR/
     DESIGN = CHOICE, POLVIEWS BY CHOICE/

BEGIN DATA
1 2 1 89
1 2 2 108
1 1 1 28
1 1 2 37
2 2 1 58
2 2 2 90
2 1 1 72
2 1 2 114
3 2 1 27
3 2 2 41
3 1 1 120
3 1 2 122
END DATA
FINISH
```

Estimates for Parameters
CHOICE

Parameter	Coeff.	Std.Err.	Z-Value
1	.0648579930	.03780	1.71592

POLVIEWS BY CHOICE

Parameter	Coeff.	Std.Err.	Z-Value
2	−.6192662223	.05598	−11.06233
3	.0494092070	.04939	1.00031

Covariance (below) and Correlation (above) Matrices of Parameter
Estimates

Parameter

	1	2	3
1	.00143	.13063	−.22366
2	.00028	.00313	−.46563
3	−.00042	−.00129	.00244

TABLE A.2
BMDP Program to Request Models Shown in Table 3.2 for Data in Table 3.1

/PROBLEM	TITLE IS 'SELECTED MODELS FOR TABLE 3.1'.
/INPUT	VARIABLES ARE 4. TABLE IS 2,2,3,4. FORMAT IS '(12F4.0)'.
/VARIABLE	NAMES ARE SEX, CHOICE, POLVIEWS, EDUC.
/TABLE	INDICES ARE SEX, CHOICE, POLVIEWS, EDUC.
/CATEGORY	NAMES (1) ARE MALE, FEMALE. CODES (1) ARE 1, 2. NAMES (2) ARE DUKA, BUSH. CODES (2) ARE 1, 2. NAMES (3) ARE LIBERAL, MODERATE, CONSERV. CODES (3) ARE 1 TO 3. NAMES (4) ARE '<12', '12', '13-15', '16 +'. CODES (4) ARE 1 TO 4.
/FIT	MODEL IS SPE, CPE, SCE, SCP. MODEL IS SPE, CPE, SCE. MODEL IS SPE, CPE, SC. MODEL IS SPE, SCE, CP. MODEL IS SPE, CPE. MODEL IS SPE, SC, CE, CP.

```
/END
12 15   7 11   9 17   7 17   6 11 16 16
14 28   7 12 19 33 21 48 14 11 27 48
17 32   9   9 19 24 28 29   3 11 36 36
46 33   5   5 11 16 16 20   4   8 41 22
/FINISH
//
```

TABLE A.3
SPSS Program for Ordinal Predictors (results are in Table 3.5)

```
DATA LIST LIST/ EDUC POLVIEWS CHOICE SEX FREQ

VALUE LABELS POLVIEWS 1 'LIBERAL' 2 'MODERATE' 3 'CONSERV'/
                      CHOICE 1 'BUSH' 2 'DUKA'/
                      SEX 1 'MALE' 2 'FEMALE'/
                      EDUC 1 '<12' 2 '12' 3 '13-15' 4 '16+'/

WEIGHT BY FREQ

COMPUTE P = POLVIEWS
COMPUTE E = EDUC
COMPUTE B = POLVIEWS * EDUC

LOGLINEAR CHOICE (1,2) BY POLVIEWS (1,3) SEX (1,2) EDUC(1,4)
                      WITH P E B/
    PRINT = ESTIM/
    DESIGN = CHOICE, CHOICE BY P, CHOICE BY E/
    DESIGN = CHOICE, CHOICE BY P, CHOICE BY E, CHOICE BY B/
BEGIN DATA
```

TABLE A.4
SAS Program for Logistic Regression of Cities Data

```
OPTIONS LS=67;
DATA NEW; SET SAVE.ALL;
PROC LOGISTIC;
MODEL MURDRATE = POP80 INCREASE V7;
```

TABLE A.5
SAS Program for Polytomous Logistic Regression in Chapter 5

```
PROC CATMOD;
DIRECT BLACK HISPANIC;
MODEL CHORES = BLACK HISPANIC/
  COVB ML NOPROFILE NOGLS;
```

TABLE A.6
SAS Program for Estimating the Ordered Logit Model in Chapter 5

```
PROC LOGISTIC;
MODEL UNSTAB = SPOUSE SPLUS/ COVB;
```

NOTES

1. The focus of this monograph is methodological rather than substantive. In light of this, the choice of predictors was motivated by a desire to keep the analysis of voting behavior relatively simple and straightforward. Political party identification, while an important factor in any model of voting preference, was not included due to the nonrecursive nature of its association with vote choice (Markus & Converse, 1979). Readers wishing a more theoretically sophisticated analysis of voting behavior in presidential elections are referred to the work of Fiorina (1981) and Nie, Verba, and Petrocik (1979).

Additionally, readers are cautioned that significance tests as reported here for the GSS may be too liberal, because standard errors were based on the assumption of simple random sampling. In that the GSS arises from a more complex sampling scheme, correct significance testing would require the calculation of adjusted standard errors. A weighted analysis, as outlined by Clogg and Eliason (1988), is one possible solution. Similar considerations apply to the National Survey of Families and Households, to be discussed later in this work.

2. This follows from the invariance property of maximum likelihood estimators, which states that the MLE for a function of a parameter is that function evaluated at the MLE for the parameter itself. That is,

$$\hat{m}_{ij} \text{ is the MLE for } m_{ij} \Rightarrow f(\hat{m}_{ij}) \text{ is the MLE for } f(m_{ij}) = \lambda.$$

3. These computations are slightly more involved because SPSS does not print either the variance of $\hat{\lambda}_{31}^{PC}$ or its covariance with the other two lambdas. Because this parameter is a linear combination of the others, however, these elements are simply functions of the variances and covariances of the first two parameter estimates. In particular,

$$\hat{\lambda}_{31}^{PC} = -(\hat{\lambda}_{11}^{PC} + \hat{\lambda}_{21}^{PC}) \Rightarrow \hat{V}(\hat{\lambda}_{31}^{PC}) = \hat{V}[-(\hat{\lambda}_{11}^{PC} + \hat{\lambda}_{21}^{PC})]$$

$$= \hat{V}(\hat{\lambda}_{11}^{PC} + \hat{\lambda}_{21}^{PC}) = \hat{V}(\hat{\lambda}_{11}^{PC}) + \hat{V}(\hat{\lambda}_{21}^{PC}) + 2\hat{\mathrm{Cov}}(\hat{\lambda}_{11}^{PC}, \hat{\lambda}_{21}^{PC}).$$

Similarly,

$$\hat{\mathrm{Cov}}(\hat{\lambda}_{31}^{PC}, \hat{\lambda}_{11}^{PC}) = \hat{\mathrm{Cov}}[-(\hat{\lambda}_{11}^{PC} + \hat{\lambda}_{21}^{PC}), \hat{\lambda}_{11}^{PC}]$$

$$= -\hat{\mathrm{Cov}}(\hat{\lambda}_{11}^{PC} + \hat{\lambda}_{21}^{PC}, \hat{\lambda}_{11}^{PC}) = -\hat{V}(\hat{\lambda}_{11}^{PC}) - \hat{\mathrm{Cov}}(\hat{\lambda}_{21}^{PC}, \hat{\lambda}_{11}^{PC}).$$

By similar covariance algebra, we have

$$\hat{\text{Cov}}\,(\lambda_{31}^{PC},\,\lambda_{21}^{PC}) = -\hat{V}\,(\lambda_{21}^{PC}) - \hat{\text{Cov}}\,(\lambda_{21}^{PC},\,\lambda_{11}^{PC})\,.$$

From these computations, we can solve for the remaining standard errors.

4. Hierarchical models are characterized by the requirement that if a higher-order term is included in a model, all its lower-order "relatives"—the lower-order effects contained within it—must also be included. In our vote choice example, if the term CPE is included in a model, then each of the two-way terms CP, CE, and PE, as well as the main effects C, P, and E, must also be in the model. A nonhierarchical model would allow one or more of these lower-order relatives to be missing. Such models make sense only in very few applications, hence they will not be considered in this monograph.

5. A model, B, is also found to be nested inside Model A if B is generated from A by placing linear constraints on the parameters in A.

6. In general, if we let $\beta_0 = \alpha$, $X_0 = 1$, and $\beta_1, \beta_2, \ldots, \beta_K$ be the logistic regression coefficients for the K predictors $X_1, X_2, \ldots, X_K$, then π_i is expressed as a function of the parameters in terms of the logistic distribution as follows:

$$\pi_i = \frac{\exp\left(\sum \beta_k X_{ki}\right)}{1 + \exp\left(\sum \beta_k X_{ki}\right)},$$

where the index of summation, k, ranges from 0 to K.

7. In general, let β represent the set of $K + 1$ parameters to be estimated in the logistic regression model. Then the likelihood function of the n independent observations y_i, $i = 1, 2, \ldots, n$, in terms of these $K + 1$ parameters, is

$$L\,(\beta, y_1, \ldots, y_n) = \prod_{i=1}^{n} \pi_i^{y_i}(1 - \pi_i)^{1 - y_i}$$

$$= \prod_{i=1}^{n} \left[\frac{\exp\left(\sum \beta_k X_{ki}\right)}{1 + \exp\left(\sum \beta_k X_{ki}\right)}\right]^{y_i} \left[\frac{1}{1 + \exp\left(\sum \beta_k X_{ki}\right)}\right]^{1 - y_i}.$$

8. Because CATMOD prints only minus twice the log likelihood for the current model, this test is not automatically provided. However, it is easily calculated by first estimating the intercepts-only model using the model statement: "MODEL CHORES = /ML NOPROFILE NOGLS." CATMOD then prints $-2 \log(L_0)$ as part of the resulting output.

REFERENCES

AGRESTI, A. (1989) "Tutorial on modeling ordered categorical response data." Psychological Bulletin 105: 290-301.

AGRESTI, A. (1990) Categorical Data Analysis. New York: John Wiley.

ALDRICH, J. H., and NELSON, F. E. (1984) Linear Probability, Logit, and Probit Models. Sage University Paper series on Quantitative Applications in the Social Sciences, 07-045. Beverly Hills, CA: Sage.

ALWIN, D. F., and HAUSER, R. M. (1975) "The decomposition of effects in path analysis." American Sociological Review 40: 37-47.

BENEDETTI, J. K., and BROWN, M. B. (1978) "Strategies for the selection of log-linear models." Biometrics 34: 680-686.

BISHOP, Y. M. M., FIENBERG, S. E., and HOLLAND, P. W. (1975) Discrete Multivariate Analysis: Theory and Practice. Cambridge: MIT Press.

BOLLEN, K. A. (1989) Structural Equations With Latent Variables. New York: John Wiley.

BOYER, R., and SAVAGEAU, D. (1981) Places Rated Almanac. Chicago: Rand McNally.

CLOGG, C. C., and ELIASON, S. R. (1988) "Some common problems in log-linear analysis," pp. 226-257 in J. S. Long (ed.) Common Problems/Proper Solutions: Avoiding Error in Quantitative Research. Newbury Park, CA: Sage.

DEMARIS, A. (1990) "Interpreting logistic regression results: A critical commentary." Journal of Marriage and the Family 52: 271-277.

DEMARIS, A. (1991) "A framework for the interpretation of first-order interaction in logit modeling." Psychological Bulletin 110: 557-570.

FIENBERG, S. E. (1980) The Analysis of Cross-Classified Categorical Data. Cambridge: MIT Press.

FIORINA, M. P. (1981) Retrospective Voting in American National Elections. New Haven, CT: Yale University Press.

HAGLE, T. M., and MITCHELL, G. E. (in press) "Goodness-of-fit measures for probit and logit." American Journal of Political Science.

HAIR, J. F., Jr., ANDERSON, R. E., and TATHAM, R. L. (1987) Multivariate Data Analysis (2nd ed.). New York: Macmillan.

HANUSHEK, E. A., and JACKSON, J. E. (1977) Statistical Methods for Social Scientists. New York: Academic Press.

HOSMER, D. W., and LEMESHOW, S. (1989) Applied Logistic Regression. New York: John Wiley.

JACCARD, J., TURRISI, R., and WAN, C. K. (1990) Interaction Effects in Multiple Regression. Sage University Paper series on Quantitative Applications in the Social Sciences, 07-072. Newbury Park, CA: Sage.

KLECKA, W. R. (1980) Discriminant Analysis. Sage University Paper series on Quantitative Applications in the Social Sciences, 07-019. Beverly Hills, CA: Sage.

LEWIS-BECK, M. S. (1980) Applied Regression: An Introduction. Sage University Paper series on Quantitative Applications in the Social Sciences, 07-022. Beverly Hills, CA: Sage.

85

MAGIDSON, J. (1981) "Qualitative variance, entropy, and correlation ratios for nominal dependent variables." Social Science Research 10: 177-194.

MARKUS, G. B., and CONVERSE, P. E. (1979) "A dynamic simultaneous equation model of electoral choice." American Political Science Review 73: 1055-1070.

McKELVEY, R. D., and ZAVOINA, W. (1975) "A statistical model for the analysis of ordinal level dependent variables." Journal of Mathematical Sociology 4: 103-120.

National Opinion Research Center (1989) General Social Surveys, 1972-1989: Cumulative Codebook. Chicago: Author.

NETER, J., WASSERMAN, W., and KUTNER, M. H. (1985) Applied Linear Statistical Models. Homewood, IL: Irwin.

NIE, N. H., VERBA, S., and PETROCIK, J. R. (1979) The Changing American Voter. Cambridge, MA: Harvard University Press.

PRESS, S. J., and WILSON S. (1978) "Choosing between logistic regression and discriminant analysis." Journal of the American Statistical Association 73: 699-705.

SPRECHER, S. (1986) "The relation between inequity and emotions in close relationships." Social Psychology Quarterly 49: 309-321.

STETS, J. E., and STRAUS, M. A. (1989) "The marriage license as a hitting license: A comparison of assaults in dating, cohabiting, and married couples," pp. 33-52 in M. A. Pirog-Good and J. E. Stets (eds.), Violence in Dating Relationships. New York: Praeger.

STEVENS, J. (1986) Applied Multivariate Statistics for the Social Sciences. Hillsdale, NJ: Lawrence Erlbaum.

SWEET, J. A., BUMPASS, L. L., and CALL, V. R. A. (1988) The Design and Content of the National Survey of Families and Households (NSFH1). Madison: University of Wisconsin, Center for Demography and Ecology.

THEIL, H. (1970) "On the estimation of relationships involving qualitative variables." American Journal of Sociology 76: 103-154.

ABOUT THE AUTHOR

ALFRED DEMARIS is currently an Associate Professor in the Department of Sociology at Bowling Green State University in Bowling Green, Ohio. He received a Ph.D. in 1982 in sociology from the University of Florida, and a master's degree in statistics in 1987 from Virginia Polytechnic Institute. His substantive interests center on the family. His articles on such topics as premarital cohabitation, marital satisfaction, and dating and marital violence have appeared in the *Journal of Marriage and the Family, Journal of Family Issues, Family Relations,* and the *Social Service Review.*